Pension Regimes and Saving

G.A. Mackenzie, Philip Gerson, and Alfredo Cuevas

INTERNATIONAL MONETARY FUND
Washington DC
August 1997

Library of Congress Cataloging-in-Publication Data

Mackenzie, G. A. (George A.), 1950–
    Pension regimes and saving / G.A. Mackenzie, Philip Gerson, and Alfred
Cuevas.
        p.   cm. — (Occasional paper ; 153)
    "September 1997."
    Includes bibliographical references (p.).
    ISBN 1-55775-640-6
    1. Pension trusts. 2. Old age pensions—FInance. 3. Saving and
Investment. 4. Defined benefit pension plans. I. Gerson, Philip R.
II. Cuevas, Alfredo. III. International Monetary Fund. IV. Title.
V. Series: Occasional paper (International Monetary Fund) ; no. 153.
HD7105.4.M23 1997
331.25'2—dc21   97-33432
                                                                                    CIP

Price: US$15.00
(US$12.00 to full-time faculty members and
students at universities and colleges)

Please send orders to:
International Monetary Fund, Publication Services
700 19th Street, N.W., Washington, D.C. 20431, U.S.A.
Tel.: (202) 623-7430   Telefax: (202) 623-7201
E-mail: publications@imf.org
Internet: http://www.imf.org

recycled paper

Contents

Appendices

The following symbols have been used throughout this paper:

...   to indicate that data are not available;

—   to indicate that the figure is zero or less than half the final digit shown, or that the item does not exist;

–   between years or months (e.g., 1994–95 or January–June) to indicate the years or months covered, including the beginning and ending years or months;

/   between years (e.g., 1994/95) to indicate a crop or fiscal (financial) year.

"Billion" means a thousand million.

Minor discrepancies between constituent figures and totals are due to rounding.

The term "country," as used in this paper, does not in all cases refer to a territorial entity that is a state as understood by international law and practice; the term also covers some territorial entities that are not states, but for which statistical data are maintained and provided internationally on a separate and independent basis.

Preface

There are few subjects in economics more topical than pensions. Public pension plans around the world are coming under fire for various perceived shortcomings. Pension expenditure has become a major burden on the public finances of many countries, both industrial and middle-income, while the payroll taxes that finance these expenditures are thought to impair the workings of labor markets and to contribute to the high rates of unemployment common among European countries.

Of particular concern to some economists has been the impact on saving and growth of pay-as-you-go public pension plans. Their establishment and expansion are thought to reduce aggregate saving in many economies, essentially because the promise of a pension after retirement encourages plan participants to reduce their voluntary saving. These and other concerns have contributed to the popularity of reforms to privatize public pension plans.

Rather than try to deal with all the facets of pension economics, this paper concentrates on the impact of pension regimes on saving, given its central importance to a country's growth prospects. It analyzes the conditions under which pension reform can increase a country's saving rate; it also considers how the development of private retirement plans can be stimulated.

The paper is a revised version of a paper prepared for the Executive Board of the International Monetary Fund. The authors received considerable assistance in its preparation. They would especially like to thank Juan Amieva for preparing the notes on Argentina, Colombia, and Peru, revised versions of which appear in Appendix III. Similarly, they thank Andrew Wolfe for his work on the note on Uruguay. Various colleagues in the IMF provided material on specific countries and helpful comments on the paper's analytical framework, including Martine Guerguil, George Kopits, and Joaquim Levy. Vito Tanzi, Peter Heller, and Teresa Ter-Minassian offered valuable overall guidance. The authors would also like to thank Scott Anderson for research assistance, and Bee Vichailak, Randa Sab, and Pearl Acquaah for secretarial assistance. Diane Cross of the Fiscal Affairs Department and Elisa Diehl of the External Relations Department edited the paper for publication, and Elisa Diehl coordinated its production.

The opinions expressed in this paper are those of the authors and should not be construed as representing the views of the IMF or of its Executive Directors.

Glossary of Abbreviations

AFORE	Administradoras de Fondos de Ahorro para el Retiro/pension company (Mexico)
AFP	Administradoras de Fondos de Pensiones/pension company (Peru)
CAJANAL	Civil Servants' Social Security Institute (Colombia)
CPF	Central Provident Fund (Singapore)
CPI	consumer price index
ERISA	Employee Retirement Income Security Act (USA)
FOVISSSTE	mandatory housing-saving fund for state workers (Mexico)
IMSS	Mexican Social Security Institute
INFONAVIT	mandatory housing-saving fund for private sector workers (Mexico)
IPSS	Peruvian Institute of Social Security
IRA	individual retirement account (USA)
ISS	Social Security Institute (Colombia)
ISSSTE	Institute for Social Security and Services for State Workers (Mexico)
IVCM	invalidez, vejez, cesantía en edad avanzada, y muerte (Mexico)
LCH	life-cycle hypothesis
OASDI	Old-Age, Survivors, and Disability Insurance (USA)
ONP	Oficina de Normalización Previsional (Peru)
PAYG	pay-as-you-go
PEMEX	Petróleos Mexicanos
PFA	Pension Fund Association (Japan)
RCV	retiro, cesantía, y vejez (Mexico)
RRSP	registered retirement savings plan (Canada)
SAR	Sistema de Ahorro para el Retiro/Individual Retirement Account (Mexico)
SSW	social security wealth

1 Introduction and Summary

Public pension reform arouses great interest virtually everywhere. In the Organization for Economic Cooperation and Development (OECD), it is generally accepted that most existing pension regimes may be financially unsustainable, and that, as the population ages, they will require substantial reform to forestall the emergence of large public sector deficits and reductions in national saving rates (see Chand and Jaeger (1996) for further discussion). High payroll tax rates necessitated by the impact of adverse demographics on public pension systems and health plans are already common in the OECD. This problem is acute in Eastern Europe, the Baltic countries, Russia, and the other countries of the former Soviet Union, although inappropriate benefit structures and administrative problems are also of great concern. In Latin America, which has had the most extensive public pension systems outside the OECD, Eastern Europe, the Baltic countries, Russia, and the other countries of the former Soviet Union, there is concern about the budgetary costs of excessively generous benefits, an eroding payroll tax base, administrative waste, and inequitable coverage and treatment. A number of countries in the region have already moved to adopt a version of the Chilean defined-contributions plan, which is privately managed.

Even in countries where the condition of the state-run schemes is less parlous, there is an ongoing debate about what role the public sector should play in the provision of pensions. The need to reform the legal and regulatory framework of private sector (occupational) pensions is a closely related concern.

Pensions can be viewed from many different angles and raise a host of issues. This paper is concerned specifically with the impact of pension regimes—and pension reform—on aggregate saving and does not pretend to be a general survey of pension economics. It can hardly be overemphasized that the basic objective of a public pension program is not to raise the saving rate, but to provide income security—at the very least, a minimum income[1]—for the elderly. The advocates of a Chilean-style reform tend to argue that it will bring about the best of both worlds: security in old age and a high saving rate.[2]

There is, nonetheless, a sense in which the issue of pensions and saving encompasses that of income security in old age because the incomes of the elderly ultimately depend on the stock of savings one generation accumulates while working and its bequest of human and physical capital to its descendants. For the same reason, the pensions and saving issue is also intimately bound up with the fiscal impact of pension reform. A pension system that promotes public sector dissaving is hardly likely to contribute to capital accumulation.

The paper's main findings and conclusions can be summarized as follows:

(1) Studies of the U.S. economy, on which most research has been done, provide some moderately strong evidence that the introduction and development of the public pension plan have depressed private sector saving, although the extent of this impact has proved hard to estimate. Studies of other countries as a group have tended to be inconclusive. In some countries, a depressing effect has been found, while studies of others have found either no significant effect or even a positive effect. The upshot is that it is not possible to generalize across countries about the impact of the public pension system on saving.

Notes: The paper uses "saving" to describe that part of current income that is not consumed, and "savings" to describe the stock of accumulated saving. The term "pensions" can cover old-age or retirement pensions, disability pensions, and survivors' (widows and orphans) pensions. This paper's primary concern is with old-age and retirement pensions, and, unless it is stated otherwise, the word "pensions" should be taken to refer to this particular class of pensions.

---

[1]It is worth remembering that there can be too much saving—the saving rate can be so high that the welfare of current generations suffers unduly, as was probably true in the Soviet Union in the 1930s.

[2]Pension system design must also be mindful of how the system treats different generations and of its impact on the distribution of income within generations. Similarly, attention needs to be paid to the way the system affects the labor market and the incentive to work.

(2) Some reasonably strong evidence exists that the growth and development of private pension plans increase private sector saving. Specifically, other private sector saving falls by less than contractual pension plan saving increases. Support for this contention is drawn largely from studies of the U.S. economy, although studies of several other countries have come to the same conclusion.

(3) Replacing a pay-as-you-go (PAYG) defined-benefits public sector plan with a defined-contributions plan along the lines of the Chilean system can increase aggregate saving. However, critically important are the contribution rates of the new plan and the means of financing the increase in the public sector deficit that characterizes the period of transition during which the old system is phased out. To maximize the impact on saving, the public sector deficit created as workers stop paying payroll taxes and start making contributions to the new system should be financed as much as possible through fiscal consolidation (e.g., tax increases or the maintenance of the payroll tax), and the contribution rate to the new system should be as high as possible.

(4) There is no compelling reason to believe that the addition of a second tier, in the form of a defined-contributions plan, to the public system should increase saving if it is financed by diverting part of the existing payroll tax from the existing system.

(5) A conventional public pension reform, which reduces the cash-flow and actuarial imbalances of the plan, will increase aggregate saving. Such a reform could comprise increases in effective retirement ages,

a reduction in the replacement ratio—the ratio of pension to salary—which can be accomplished in a number of ways, or increases in contribution rates. This kind of reform of the existing system, which does not entail a fundamental change in the way it is managed or administered, increases aggregate saving because it increases public sector saving without entailing a fully offsetting decline in private sector saving. That said, any measures to increase public sector saving should boost total saving because such increases are typically not fully offset by a decline in private sector saving. Conceivably, even the announcement of *future* declines in the replacement ratio could prompt an increase in private saving.

(6) A drastic increase in saving in the short run deriving from a conventional public pension reform would probably require either a major reduction in the real value of the pensions of the current generation of pensioners or large hikes in payroll tax rates. Gradual changes in the pension regime, desirable as they are from the point of view of the welfare of the current generation of pensioners, would take years to boost the saving rate significantly.

(7) The spread of private pension regimes may well increase aggregate saving. There is, however, no reliable way of encouraging a speedy increase in the coverage of the private pension system, except, possibly, through tax incentives. The depressing impact of such incentives on public sector saving may, however, outweigh the positive impact on private sector saving of broader private pension plan coverage.

II   Pension Regimes and Saving— A Framework for Analysis

How a pension regime affects saving depends crucially on its basic design (Box 1; Table 1), as well as on the forces and influences that motivate saving by individuals.[3] The life-cycle hypothesis (LCH) of consumption, although somewhat extreme in its assumptions (and implications), has become the standard vehicle for analyzing the saving decision.[4] This paper uses it as the starting point for its discussion.

In its simplest form, the LCH implies that consumption is a function only of lifetime wealth.[5] It is not affected by changes in the pattern of income over time. Provided that wealth—defined to include not only financial and real assets (the traditional accounting definition), but also the expected value of future income from labor (human capital wealth)—does not change, neither should the pattern of consumption over time. Because consumption does not fluctuate (or fluctuate much) with disposable income, the propensity to save out of disposable income will vary over an individual's life. It will be high in the prime earning years and low or negative in retirement.

The LCH has a remarkable implication for pension system design. Unless pension reform alters the wealth of pension plan participants, it will not affect consumption. It may affect the distribution of saving between the public and the private sector, but not its total amount. For example, an increase in contributions to a funded public pension plan may lead to an increase in public sector saving, but this will be exactly offset by a fall in private sector saving.

The LCH implies that pension reform can affect the saving rate in one or more of three ways: (1) by affecting the average wealth of plan participants; (2) by redistributing wealth between different age groups, which will have different propensities to save; and (3) by redistributing wealth among members of the same age group with different propensities to save.

The LCH in its simplest and most extreme form, however, rests on strong and basically implausible assumptions about human behavior and financial markets. Capital markets are far from being as perfect as the LCH requires. Even in countries where these markets are well developed, individuals normally require physical collateral (e.g., a residential dwelling) to borrow substantial sums of money. Interest rates on unsecured loans are typically much higher than the rates on short-term financial assets, so that consuming on the strength of future income becomes expensive, and credit limits are in any case stricter. Even in the United States, with its highly developed financial markets, comparatively few elderly people purchase annuities, probably because these cannot be had on even moderately favorable terms (Warshawsky, 1987). Indexed annuities are extremely rare, as are indexed occupational pensions.[6] These problems are compounded in countries where financial markets are less well developed.

Capital market imperfections aside, a person who cannot rely on the support of an extended family in old age and who tries to determine how much to save for retirement is confronted with what can be a bewilderingly complex decision. When we decide between "jam today" and "jam tomorrow," the information at our disposal is clearly limited: unlike the choice between tea today and coffee today, the experience of old age cannot be repeated. This uncertainty about the future can lead some people to save too much, but it is doubtful that most are so farsighted as to be able to save enough to maintain their accustomed standard of living in old age. Indeed, the

---

[3]The framework outlined here has typically been used to analyze public pension systems, but applies to private pension regimes as well.

[4]See, for example, Auerbach and Kotlikoff (1995) and Blanchard and Fischer (1989).

[5]Saving would also be a function of the interest rate—the relative price of consumption now compared with consumption in the future. Studies of saving typically find it is not elastic with respect to the rate of interest.

[6]Diamond (1996), in a discussion of the feasibility of a Chilean-style reform in the United States, notes (p. 83) "to date, there are no privately provided annuities indexed to the . . . CPI, so these would need to be developed. . . .[this] would probably need CPI-indexed Treasury securities. . . ." These are now being issued.

Table 1. Selected Countries: Basic Features of Public Pension Schemes

Country	Degree of Funding	Type	Form of Benefit	Maximum Replacement Ratio (in percent)	Indexation (index, degree, and frequency)	Redistributive Element	Coverage (in percent of economically active population)	Financing Source	Pension Expenditure (in percent of GDP) and Year
Argentina	N	DB	A, B	N/A	O, A	Yes	56%	PT, GR[2]	5.4 1994
Australia (old)	N/A	DB	A, FR	25% of average wage	CPI, F, B	No	100%	GR	3.8 1989
Australia (new)[3]	F	DC	A, ER	N/A	N/A	Yes	100%	PT	N/A
Canada[4]	N	DB	A, ER	25% of max. pensionable earnings	CPI, F, A[5]	No	100%	PT	3.8 1990
Chile (new)	F	DC	B, IER	N/A	CPI, F	Yes	Broad	C	5.7[6] 1989
Colombia (old)	N	DB	A, ER	85%[7]	W, F, A	Yes	30%	PT	2.3 1993
France	N	DB	A, ER	50%[8]	CPI, F	Yes	100%	PT	11.9 1992
Germany	N	DB	A, ER	70% (average)	W, F, A	Yes, modest	Universal	PT	8.9 1992
Israel	N	DB	A, B	30%	W, F	Yes	Universal	PT	5.0 1989
Italy	N	DB	A, B	80%	CPI, F, A	Yes, significant	Universal	PT, GR	13.9 1990
Japan	P	DB	A, B	N/A	W, F, A	Yes	Universal	PT, GR	5.0 1990
Peru	N	DB	ER	100%	W[9]	Yes	30%	PT, GR	0.7 1986
Singapore	F	DC	B, IER	N/A	N/A	No	Universal	C	2.2 1989
South Africa	N/A	DB	A, FR	N/A	CPI, F, A	Yes	Universal	GR	N/A
Spain	N	DB	A, B	80%	CPI, F, A	Yes, significant	Universal	PT, GR	9.2[10] 1995
Sweden[4]	P	DB	A, ER	60% (ER component)	CPI, F, A	Yes	Universal	PT	7.0 1990
Switzerland[11]	N	DB	A, B	40% of average wage	Index[12]	Yes	Universal	PT, GR	10.1 1992
Turkey	N	DB	A, B	85%	CPI, F, B	Yes	Universal	PT, GR[13]	2.4 1986
United Kingdom	N	DB	A, B	25% for earnings	CPI, A	Yes	Nearly 100%	PT, GR	4.2 1990
United States	P	DB	A, ER	41% of average wage[14]	CPI, A	Yes, significant	Universal	PT	4.5 1990
Uruguay (old)[15]	N	DB	B, ER	80%	W, F, Q	Yes, significant	80%	PT, GR[16]	13.0 1994
Uruguay (new private)	F	DC	B	N/A	N/A	N/A	N/A	PT	N/A
Uruguay (new public)	N	DB	B, ER	80%	W, F, three times annually	Yes, significant	N/A	PT, GR[16]	N/A

Sources: World Bank; Organization for Economic Cooperation and Development; country authorities; and U.S. Social Security Administration.

Notes: Degree of funding
 Partial (P)
 Full (F)
 None (N)
Type of plan
 Defined benefits (DB)
 Defined contributions (DC)
Form of benefit
 Lump sum (LS) or annuity (A) or both (B)
 Flat rate (FR) or earnings-related (ER) or both (B); or indirectly earnings-related (IER)(the case of defined-contributions plan)
Indexation
 Index: CPI, wages (W), other (O)
 Degree: partial (P), full (F)
 Frequency: Annual (A)
  Biannual (B)
  Quarterly (Q)

Financing source
  Payroll tax (PT)
  General revenues (GR)
  Contribution (C)
  Other (O)

[1] Indexation of pensions to average contribution (AMPO) was suspended by the Social Security Solidarity Law in early 1995.
[2] Under the revenue-sharing arrangement, a part of tax revenues is earmarked for social security.
[3] New system budgeted in 1995—to be phased in by 1998.
[4] ER scheme only.
[5] For existing pensioners.
[6] State and privatized.
[7] The replacement ratio cannot exceed 85 percent of the worker's salary or 20 minimum wages.
[8] Basic pension (régime général).
[9] Usually adjusted with central government wages.
[10] Projected.
[11] First tier only.
[12] Every two years, or when index—a simple average of CPI and wage index—increases over 8 percent (whichever comes first).
[13] General revenues, if deficit.
[14] But declines with income.
[15] New system took effect January 1, 1996.
[16] Includes earmarked taxes.

Box 1. Basic Features of Public Pension Plans

A number of basic features of public pension plans have a bearing on their impact on saving.

Public pension plans may be either *unfunded PAYG, partially funded, or fully funded*. Most public plans are either PAYG or partially funded (e.g., Japan). The plans of Chile and Singapore, which are fully funded, are notable exceptions (see Box 2). With PAYG plans, current revenue is expected to finance current pension obligations, and the rate of the payroll tax—the standard financing source for public pension plans—is adjusted from time to time to ensure that revenues and expenditures balance. Reserves are maintained only to finance temporary or cyclical shortfalls in revenue. Under a funded plan, the rate should in principle be set initially at a level that is expected to ensure that the plan will always be self-financing (i.e., so that no subsequent increase in the rate will be required). This implies that the expected present value of benefits equals the expected present value of contributions over an essentially indefinite period.

A related distinction is between *defined-benefits* and *defined-contributions* plans. The former typically defines plan participants' benefits as a function of salary and work history. Letting P equal the value of the pension, N the number of years of coverage, Y pensionable income, and b a constant, one fairly standard formulation for an earnings-related pension is $P = bYN$ (with N typically subject to a maximum of 30–35 years). Y is usually an average of income over some subperiod within the contribution period, generally near the end of working life.

A defined-contributions plan does not define the benefit; plan participants, upon retirement, get back their contributions plus their accumulated return, with the pension benefit taking the form of one lump-sum payment or a series of lump-sum payments or an annuity. Most public pension plans are defined-benefits plans rather than defined-contributions plans; Chile and Singapore are, again, exceptions. A defined-contributions plan is fully funded by definition; if its investment experience is poor, the average pension benefit will be reduced. A defined-benefits plan may be either funded to some degree or unfunded. Its "fundedness" is never perfect, in that any calculation of the actuarial soundness of a plan is based on uncertain assumptions, especially as to the rate of return to plan assets.

Pension benefits may take the form of an *annuity* (typically, although not always, a life annuity with some right of survivorship) or a *lump sum*, or a mix. The U.S. Old-Age, Survivor, and Disability Insurance (OASDI) system provides a life annuity with survivors' benefits. Under Singapore's Central Provident Fund (CPF), which is a defined-contributions plan, retiring participants can withdraw all of their account in one lump sum, except for a set amount (about $21,500 in 1993) that must be used to finance a fixed monthly pension.

Benefits may be either *flat rate* or *earnings related*. Until recently, Australia's plan provided only a flat-rate benefit, although the benefit was means tested. Many plans have a flat-rate and an earnings-related component (Japan, United Kingdom). Any plan with a minimum pension has a flat-rate element to it over a certain income range. Finally, pension plans may or may not have a *redistributive component*. Pensions that are solely earnings related do not, unless the replacement ratio varies inversely with income level. In practice, most earnings-related pension plans do have a redistributive component because most have some combination of minimum and maximum pensions and contribution levels.

The degree and modalities of *indexation* of a pension annuity are important features that vary substantially across countries. The U.S. system and that of a few other countries now offer full indexation to the consumer price index (CPI). Some countries have legislated an indexation provision without having been able to honor it on a timely basis (e.g., Argentina prior to the reforms of the early 1990s, and Bolivia, Mexico, and Peru at various times during the 1980s).

A basic feature of a pension plan is its *replacement ratio*, which is the ratio of the pension benefit to some measure of income earned during the contribution period. This parameter should be known in a defined-benefits plan that can honor its promises; a defined-contributions plan, by definition, cannot guarantee any particular replacement ratio.

Last, the macroeconomic implications of public pension plans depend on their relative size. In addition to the replacement ratio, their size depends on the extent of their *coverage*, namely, the share of the working-age population eligible to contribute, or some similar indicator. Also important is the *degree of maturity* of the plan. Immature plans are those that have not yet reached their full size or their long-term dependency ratio—the ratio of pensioners to contributors—because the current generation of retired persons will not have contributed long enough (if at all) to qualify for a full pension. The plans of all industrial countries have more or less universal coverage and are already mature. The plans of the Southern Cone countries are also mature. Their coverage is quite broad but not universal.

The finances of PAYG plans are affected heavily by maturation and by underlying demographic trends because the equilibrating contribution rate varies directly with the ratio of retired to working-age persons—the dependency ratio.

If the average pension is B, the payroll tax rate t, the number of contributors L, the contributions base (the average wage) W, and the number of pensioners P, cash-flow equilibrium of a PAYG plan requires the following: $BP = tWL$; or, $t = (P/L)(B/W)$. Thus, the required contribution rate varies directly with the dependency ratio (P/L) and the average replacement rate (B/W).

traditional arguments for publicly provided pensions include the assertions that savings vehicles are inadequate and that much of the population will need to be protected from its own improvidence.[7]

---

[7]See Barr (1993). When a significant share of the population is improvident, compulsory saving plans can be justified as a means of surmounting the free-rider problem that is created when society feels an obligation to support the destitute elderly, whether or not they have attempted to make adequate provision for their old age. As regards savings vehicles, in many developing countries, real rates of return on savings deposits and other instruments have been negative on average for lengthy periods of time, although the trend toward financial liberalization has made such poor rates of return less common.

To summarize, even if the extreme version of the LCH were to apply, pension regimes could affect the saving rate by affecting the wealth of plan participants. As explained below, PAYG schemes can affect participants' wealth by creating what has come to be known as social security wealth (SSW). A fortiori, when capital markets are imperfect and plan participants must make complicated choices in conditions of great uncertainty, other channels of influence are opened. As a result, when public pension plans are introduced, it may not be possible for their contributors to maintain the same level of consumption.

III Public Pension Plans, Their Reform, and Saving

This section describes how public pension plans could be expected, on a priori grounds, to affect saving. It uses the LCH only as a starting point and acknowledges the implications of imperfect capital markets and imperfect information about the future. Three cases are presented: (1) Introduction of a PAYG plan where no plan existed previously. The literature invariably covers such cases, and the conclusions are relevant for the many countries that are contemplating a substantial expansion of an existing plan with narrow coverage. (2) Incremental reform to an established PAYG plan with universal coverage. (3) Introduction of a defined-contributions plan. Some of the main findings of this section are illustrated mathematically in Appendix I.

Introducing a Pay-as-You-Go Plan

A PAYG plan can conceivably redistribute wealth from generations with a high saving propensity to generations with a low saving propensity. The first retirees under the new scheme often enjoy a very high implicit rate of return to their contributions—and thus an increase in their wealth—because eligibility conditions are generous and contribution rates are low.[8] In effect, the first retirees benefit from a windfall—they receive a quantity of SSW that may be very large compared with their existing wealth. Because retirees are at the stage where they are running down their asset holdings and because their wealth has increased, their consumption expenditure will also increase.

What of the members of the current working generation? The imposition of a payroll tax will reduce their disposable income, but offsetting this effect is the promise of a retirement pension. If the implicit rate of return to their payroll tax contributions is high enough, the people currently working will act as if their wealth has not declined. Hence, according to the strict version of the LCH, they will not reduce their consumption spending, but will instead reduce their voluntary saving. In these circumstances, introducing a PAYG plan will depress saving: both private sector and aggregate saving will fall.[9] The capital stock is permanently reduced by the impact of the windfall received by the first generation of retirees, even though only the initial generation of retirees really benefits from the introduction of the PAYG scheme.[10] Subsequent generations do not receive a windfall, but may be led to believe that they will not have to provide for themselves, or at least not to the same extent, in retirement.

The impact of the substantial SSW created for the first generation of retirees can, however, be countered, at least partially, through compensating transfers between the affected generations. For example, the current working generation may spend less of its own money on caring for its parents because their income from social security has risen, or the elderly may increase their bequests or inter vivos transfers to their children. There is evidence that a "bequest" motive underlies much saving (Kotlikoff and Summers, 1981). Nonetheless, these transfers do not extinguish SSW; they simply transfer it across generations.

The increase in the wealth of those plan participants nearing retirement can also, paradoxically, increase saving if the increase in wealth resulting from the introduction of the PAYG plan prompts a desire for early retirement, and thus a need for supplementary savings (Feldstein, 1974; Munnell, 1976). The increase in wealth enjoyed by persons close to retirement can mean, for example, that by saving a little more, they can retire early without either suffering

---

[8]The implicit rate of return is the rate that equates the present expected value of contributions with the present expected value of pension benefits. The high implicit rate of return enjoyed by the early participants in the OASDI scheme in the United States is well documented (Duggan, Gillingham, and Greenlees, 1993). If the implicit rate of return equals the market rate of interest, no net SSW is created.

[9]This view is associated with Feldstein (1974).

[10]Subsequent generations also experience an increase in wealth from participation in the pension system to the extent that the implicit rate of return on their contributions exceeds the interest rate. The implicit rate of return may well become negative, however.

an undue decline in retirement income or having to depress drastically their pre-retirement level of consumption.

The impact on saving of the introduction of a PAYG plan is also conditioned by the effects of capital market imperfections and the shortsightedness that often overcomes people making decisions in the face of an uncertain and distant future. The presence of myopia and capital market imperfections means both that people save too little and that they are income constrained. In consequence, their saving rate may be so low that they cannot maintain their level of consumption by lowering saving to pay for the payroll tax contributions that finance the PAYG scheme, and they will have difficulty borrowing to sustain their original level of consumption. They will also discount future pension benefits heavily. In these circumstances, the impact of the SSW windfall bestowed on early retirees is muted.[11]

Even if people are more farsighted and save more, social security "saving" will not be equivalent to voluntary private saving. Social security saving is "locked up" until retirement and cannot function as a vehicle for precautionary saving, as can short-term bank deposits or other financial investments. This too will attenuate the depressing effect of the SSW windfall on saving.

Apart from the difference in liquidity between voluntary saving and involuntary social security saving, there is a question as to how social security contributions are viewed by plan participants. If they are viewed as a form of saving—albeit involuntary and long term—that earns an adequate rate of return in the form of the expected future stream of pension benefits, then they are more likely to substitute for voluntary saving. Contributors are most likely to adopt this view of the payroll tax when contributions and benefits are tightly linked.

But the link can be weak when there is a redistributive element in the pension plan, like ceilings or floors. For example, with a flat-rate pension, there is little or no relationship between the value of contributions and the value of the pension.[12] The increase in payroll tax contributions that results when wages and salaries increase does not lead to an automatic increase in future benefits. In this case, there is no

reason to expect substitution of voluntary savings for increased payroll tax contributions.[13]

Even when the legal structure of the system entails a tight link, that link can be virtually destroyed by episodes of financial instability. In many countries, the social security system has been unable to maintain the replacement ratio stipulated by law, at least in real terms. Adverse demographic trends have contributed to this phenomenon, even when financial conditions have been stable. It is, in fact, common for the replacement ratio to be set at high levels at the outset of the retirement period, only to fall more or less continuously thereafter. It is not uncommon for the real value of a retirement pension to be highly variable, as it has been in countries experiencing hyperinflationary episodes. These elements of uncertainty can be expected to reduce the substitutability of social security for private saving.

It should not be surprising that the empirical evidence is hard to interpret, given the theoretical ambiguity of the impact of pension regimes on saving; the ways this impact can be conditioned by the economic, institutional, and social environment; and the substantial statistical problems researchers have stumbled across in testing for a relationship (see Appendix II for a fuller treatment of the empirical literature). In the United States, where most studies have been conducted, to the extent that a consensus exists, it is that social security has depressed private saving to some degree, although the offset effect is significantly less than 100 percent. In other countries, the results are mixed. SSW effects have been found in Italy and Japan, for example, but not in Canada, France, or the United Kingdom.

Reforming Existing Pay-as-You-Go Plans

When a mature PAYG system with broad coverage is already in place, the transitional impact, if any, has worked its way through. The impact of the SSW windfall on the first generation of retirees will be largely water over the dam (although the private sector saving rate will remain lower than it was previously), because subsequent generations will not enjoy an unusually high implicit rate of return. Nonetheless, changes to the structure of the existing system can in principle affect the saving rate, and the way they affect it will depend on the characteristics of financial

---

[11]Another effect can be present when annuities are not available on reasonably favorable terms. Then, the introduction of a pension plan can be seen as reducing the risk of living so long after retirement that one's savings are exhausted. In this case, the lessened risk can exercise a depressing effect on saving.

[12]There may be some relationship, to the extent that to be eligible a potential beneficiary must work and contribute for a certain number of years. However, there will be no relationship between average salary during the qualifying period and the value of the pension, and extensions of the contributory period will not increase that value.

[13]If a plan has a ceiling on contributions and a maximum pension benefit that are set deliberately to impart a redistributive component to the system, as with the U.S. OASDI program, there is a range of incomes over which a tight link is established. Once income exceeds a certain level, the link is broken. Contributions increase, but future benefits do not. Providing a flat-rate pension may lead to a reduction in saving, but the size of the decline will not vary with income.

markets and saving behavior already noted. Before considering the more radical reform represented by the adoption of a defined-contributions plan, it is important to consider how incremental or piecemeal reforms will affect an existing PAYG system.

Reform affects two separate groups of people: the current generation of pensioners and current working contributors.

Current Pensioners

A reduction in the real value of the average pension will probably increase the sum total of public and private sector saving. Pensioners' income has to fall unless transfers from family members compensate for the reduction. This kind of approach to reform is extreme and may be seen as unfair because it breaks the implicit contract made with pensioners while they were working. Nonetheless, it can raise the saving rate. The increase in public sector saving that results from the reduction in transfer payments should not be fully offset by the fall in private saving that takes place as pensioners or their families attempt to sustain the pensioners' level of consumption. A full offset is unlikely because the perceived wealth of the private sector as a whole (and, perhaps more important, its current income) will have fallen.[14]

Current Participants and Future Pensioners

An increase in saving that results from reform must derive from either a reduction in the average expected pension or an increase in contributions. Pensions may be reduced by reducing the accrual rate; lowering the base of pensionable income; and increasing the age or number of years of plan participation at which the maximum pension is achieved.

All of these measures can reduce the average expected pension of future retirees. Moreover, as these measures take effect, they reduce private sector disposable income.[15] A reduction in the accrual rate, unless it is retroactive, will affect the flow of pensions only very gradually.[16] A reduction in the pen-

sionable base (e.g., making pensions a function of the average annual salary of, say, the last 15 years rather than the last 4) can have a much more draconian effect, but the sudden imposition of such a change can be seen as unfair. The same is true of the third option.

Nonetheless, any of these measures will reduce the expected future income of the current working generation unless it has been anticipated. If perceived wealth is reduced, and there is no change to the retirement age, the current working generation will have to save more to attain the same standard of living in retirement. In this case, both private and public saving can increase.[17]

An increase in the contribution rate will lower the disposable income of contributors because the effective incidence of the payroll tax, whatever its legal incidence, falls mostly on labor. This reduction in disposable income will presumably reduce both perceived wealth and consumption unless the increase in the rate is seen as financing a higher pension down the road. Private saving may fall, but the sum of public and private saving will rise. The high level of contributions in most countries where social security coverage is broad, and the need to avoid exacerbating labor market problems, however, argues against further rate increases in most countries.[18]

How much extra saving can be generated through incremental reform along these lines? It is generally accepted that measures to increase public sector saving will not be wholly offset by a decline in private saving (conceivably, private saving may even increase). By combining projections of the impact of reform on the pension plan's accounts with an assumption about the impact of increased public saving on private saving, one can derive an illustrative range of estimates of the impact of incremental reform on saving.

Projections for the public pension systems of Canada, France, Germany, and Sweden show a clear tendency toward increasing cash-flow deficits in the absence of reform.[19] These tendencies can be arrested through various changes to the structure of benefits (Table 2). The most potent change is a

---

[14]This kind of policy, by weakening confidence in the public pension system, could stimulate private saving. Repeated recourse to it would, however, tend to defeat the purpose of a public pension scheme. The analysis assumes that the reduction in the public sector deficit is not used to finance tax cuts or expenditure increases.

[15]The *introduction* of a PAYG system, in contrast, has no effect on private sector disposable income.

[16]For example, suppose the accrual rate is 0.02, which means that for each extra year an individual works, the pension increases by 2 percent of the pensionable income base. If the rate is reduced to 0.015, it will take ten years for the replacement rate of *new* retirees to drop by 5 percentage points, and the *average* replacement rate will scarcely be affected. Nonetheless, this change in the accrual rate will entail a big decline in the *steady-state* replacement rate—from 70 percent for a 35-year working life to 52.5 percent.

[17]This is not a foregone conclusion, given that saving behavior will depend on, among other considerations, how farsighted people are. Although perceived wealth is reduced, there is no substitution effect—the return to private saving is unaffected. Rather than let consumption in retirement fall by the full extent of the decline in the pension, current workers will reduce pre-retirement consumption (i.e., pre-retirement saving will be increased) if consumption both before and after retirement is positively related to wealth.

[18]The argument that payroll taxation is distortional requires the assumption that at least part of the incidence of the payroll tax is on employers.

[19]The projections are based on those described in Chand and Jaeger (1996).

Table 2. Selected Countries: Impact of Reform on Public Pension Plans[1]
(In percent of GDP)

	1995	1996	1997	1998	1999	2000	2005	2010	2015
France									
Baseline balance	−0.5	−0.4	−0.3	−0.2	−0.1	0.0	0.6	−0.4	−2.7
Scenario 1	1.1	1.1	1.2	1.2	1.3	1.4	1.6	2.1	2.8
Scenario 2	0.3	0.3	0.3	0.4	0.4	0.5	0.7	1.3	1.9
Scenario 3	0.0	0.1	0.1	0.2	0.3	0.4	0.7	1.1	1.5
Scenario 4	0.0	0.1	0.3	0.4	0.5	0.7	1.3	2.0	2.7
Scenario 5	1.2	1.7	2.3	2.5	3.3	4.1	4.4	6.3	8.5
Canada									
Baseline balance	−0.2	−0.2	−0.2	−0.3	−0.4	−0.5	−0.8	−1.4	−2.4
Scenario 1	0.4	0.5	0.5	0.5	0.5	0.5	0.7	0.9	1.2
Scenario 2	0.2	0.3	0.3	0.3	0.3	0.3	0.6	0.8	1.1
Scenario 3[2]	0.0	0.0	0.0	0.0	0.0	0.0	0.0	0.0	0.0
Scenario 4	0.1	0.1	0.1	0.2	0.2	0.3	0.4	0.5	0.7
Scenario 5	0.5	0.6	0.6	0.6	0.6	0.6	0.7	1.2	1.6
Germany									
Baseline balance	0.2	0.0	−0.2	−0.5	−0.7	−0.9	−1.0	−1.3	−2.6
Scenario 1	1.0	1.1	1.2	1.4	1.4	1.5	1.9	2.3	2.9
Scenario 2	0.2	0.3	0.4	0.5	0.6	0.7	1.1	1.7	2.3
Scenario 3	0.3	0.6	0.8	1.1	1.4	1.6	2.7	3.6	4.3
Scenario 4	0.4	0.6	0.9	1.2	1.5	1.8	3.0	4.2	5.1
Scenario 5	1.7	1.9	2.1	2.4	2.5	2.6	2.2	2.1	2.5
Sweden									
Baseline balance	1.3	0.3	0.3	0.3	0.4	0.4	0.7	0.2	−0.8
Scenario 1	1.1	1.2	1.3	1.3	1.3	1.4	1.8	2.3	2.9
Scenario 2	0.3	0.4	0.5	0.6	0.6	0.6	1.4	1.9	2.5
Scenario 3[2]	0.0	0.0	0.0	0.0	0.0	0.0	0.0	0.0	0.0
Scenario 4	0.0	0.1	0.1	0.2	0.2	0.2	0.6	1.0	1.6
Scenario 5	1.0	1.0	1.0	1.1	1.0	1.1	1.5	2.1	2.7

Notes: Scenario 1. Change in balance as a percent of GDP assuming a decrease in the replacement rate of 5 percentage points for all pensions.
Scenario 2. Change in balance as a percent of GDP assuming a decrease in the replacement rate of 5 percentage points for new pensions.
Scenario 3. Change in balance as a percent of GDP assuming full indexation to the CPI.
Scenario 4. Change in balance as a percent of GDP assuming 80 percent indexation to the CPI.
Scenario 5. Change in balance as a percent of GDP assuming a front-loaded increase in the retirement age to 67 years.
[1]Scenarios include impact of pension reform on public sector interest payments and receipts.
[2]Canada's and Sweden's baselines are already indexed to the CPI.

marked reduction in the replacement rate that affects existing and new pensioners alike. Thus, for example, the balance of Germany's pension plan increases by 1.9 percent of GDP between 1995 and 2005, when the replacement rate is lowered by 5 percentage points for all pensioners (entailing a decline in the average pension of about 10 percent). Assuming that the offset factor for private saving is 50 percent, the impact on the saving rate over this ten-year period will be about 1 percent of GDP. In Canada, where the replacement rate is lower, the impact on the balance of the system of a similar adjustment will be 0.7 percent of GDP over the same period. With the same offset factor for private saving, the impact on aggregate saving will be 0.4 percent.

Reforms that affect the number of new pensioners in a given period and the average pension these pensioners receive may ultimately reduce the replacement ratio substantially. Initially, however, the reforms will have only a modest impact on aggregate saving. Thus, the same 5 percentage point reduction in replacement rates in Germany—but for new pensioners only—will initially increase public saving by only 0.2 percent of GDP. Its impact on the public sector deficit will increase to 1.1 percent by 2005 and reach 2.3 in 2015. The initial impact of an increase in the effective retirement age must be greater than that of a reduction in the replacement rate for new pensioners because, assuming no change in the retirement age, it will be tantamount to a 100 percent reduction in the replacement rate for new pensioners.[20]

These illustrative simulations of mature pension systems with aging populations also suggest lessons for countries contemplating a substantial increase in the coverage of an existing PAYG system. These countries are probably best advised to ensure that the terms of benefits are not excessively generous, so that politically unpalatable increases in contribution rates do not become necessary as the system matures further. A range of reforms may be required, including increases in the effective retirement age, a reduction in the accrual rate, and a redefinition of the base of pensionable income. In addition, the plan's finances should be based on conservative demographic assumptions so that the risk of unforeseen increases in the dependency ratio is minimized. These procedures, together with administrative reform where necessary, will at least minimize the risk of reducing public sector saving. They may also entail forsaking a strictly PAYG system for a partially if not a fully funded system. The degree of funding achieved will depend on, among other factors, the impact of reform on average replacement ratios and contribution rates.

Introducing a Defined-Contributions Plan

The effects on saving arising from the introduction of a defined-contributions plan will be heavily dependent on whether the plan is intended to replace an existing PAYG system and on the modalities of its introduction. To begin with, it is useful to analyze the potential effects of the introduction of a compulsory defined-contributions plan, assuming for the sake of the exposition that no PAYG plan is already in place.

When No Pay-as-You-Go System Is in Place

A defined-contributions plan is essentially a compulsory saving plan, so that contributors, upon retirement, get back only what they put in, plus the accumulated return on their investment. Given that the present value of expected pension benefits should equal the present value of contributions at the market rate of interest, no net SSW is created, and there is thus no intergenerational wealth effect. An intergenerational wealth effect is created, however, if the

return to contributions is artificially subsidized by the government, and may occur in the presence of imperfect capital markets and myopic plan contributors.

Consequently, the establishment of a defined-contributions plan should not reduce saving. At worst, it will simply result in a fully offsetting reduction in voluntary saving. It can increase saving, however, when the contribution rate is above the rate at which participants would save if left to their own devices and if capital market imperfections inhibit borrowing on the strength of future income. This increase is more likely to materialize when the conditions for withdrawing the funds are comparatively strict, as in Chile, where contributors may withdraw funds only upon retirement. Singapore's CPF now allows contributors substantial withdrawals to finance the purchase of a house and home insurance, medical expenses, and certain types of savings accounts (Box 2).[21] Thus, an account with the CPF is far more substitutable with liquid financial assets than an account with a Chilean pension fund. A number of studies of saving in Singapore and of the substitutability between voluntary saving and saving through the CPF have not as yet produced a consensus on this issue, however.[22]

When a Pay-as-You-Go Plan Is in Place

The state-regulated defined-contributions plan in Chile was introduced alongside a quite extensive PAYG system (Box 2). Participation in the new system was optional for persons already contributing to one of the state-run funds, but fresh entrants to the labor market (young workers), if not self-employed, were and are required to participate. The state-run system will be phased out automatically as the remaining contributors gradually retire and die. In this respect, the Chilean reform differs from the reforms implemented subsequently by Peru and Argentina. In Peru, participation in the new plan was optional even for new labor market participants. In Argentina, the defined-contributions plan was added as a second tier on top of the existing state-run system; simultaneously, a number of changes were made to the first tier with a view to improving its finances. (See

---

[20]The very large longer-term impact projected from an increase in the retirement age in France to 67 years results mainly from the current low effective age of retirement and from the impact of the deficit reduction on public sector interest payments (Table 2).

[21]In comparison, Malaysia's provident fund allows substantial withdrawals at age 50 and for critical illnesses.

[22]A recent IMF publication found that there was strong substitutability (Husain, 1995). The imperfect substitutability of a Chilean-style pension account with liquid financial assets may explain why participation of the self-employed (which is voluntary) remains low in the Chilean plan. Saving for a house or for a commercial investment may seem far more attractive to young adults than participation in a retirement plan. See Gillion and Bonilla (1992).

Box 2. Two Pioneers in Pension Reform

Chile

Chile's privately managed, publicly regulated plan was introduced in 1981. Participation was voluntary for persons already contributing to the state system, but obligatory for first-time employees. Nonetheless, the combined effect of participation in the new plan by new labor market entrants and substantial migration from the state system has raised the coverage of the new system to over 90 percent of the labor force, although only about 60 percent of these contribute regularly.

Participants pay a contribution that is a fixed percentage of their gross salary to an account registered in their name with the pension fund of their choice, as well as a management fee with a fixed percentage and a flat component. Some 21 funds were operating as of end-1994. Switches between funds cost the contributor nothing. The funds' administrative costs, which include sales commissions, are high compared with large, well-administered public schemes. Average returns on contributors' accounts have been high, reflecting, among other things, the government's policy of indexing financial assets. With the development of Chile's capital market and the advent of financial stability, the range of assets in which pension funds may invest has been broadened.

Upon retirement—the standard age is 65 for men and 60 for women—contributors may choose among several combinations of lump-sum payments (programmed withdrawals) and annuities (which are indexed); at present, the former is the preferred choice. Given the age of the system, comparatively few persons have retired.

Singapore

Singapore's Central Provident Fund (CPF) was established in 1955 and is a fully funded individual account system, with lump-sum and annuity benefits; there is no redistributive aspect. It currently covers about three-fourths of the population. Contribution rates in 1994 were 20 percent each for employers and employees and were capped at a monthly salary level of S$6,000 (US$4,000). The government does not contribute, except in its capacity as an employer. By law, virtually all the assets of the CPF are invested in government bonds, and the proceeds of the bond sales are mainly invested abroad.

After reaching the age of 55, members may withdraw as a lump sum all but a fixed amount (S$34,600 in 1993), which is used to finance a fixed monthly pension payable at age 60. Although the starting amount of this pension is indexed to the CPI, the pension for an individual is not indexed once it commences, and ceases once the individual exhausts the fixed sum plus accumulated interest (after about 14 years). A member's account is fully portable. Since 1968, when accounts were just a source of pension income, withdrawal privileges have been steadily expanded. Now, withdrawals are allowed for housing, medical, education, and home insurance expenses and for investing in certain types of savings assets. Employee contributions and all withdrawals are excluded from taxable income, as are interest earnings on member balances.

Appendix III for a further discussion of the reforms in Peru and Argentina.)

One of the often-cited benefits of the Chilean reform is its apparently beneficial effect on capital market development. A defined-contributions plan can have an impact on capital markets because it generates a surplus that must be invested. Even if voluntary saving is reduced by exactly the amount of the saving channeled to the defined-contributions plan—as might occur if the defined-contributions plan were introduced as a supplementary second tier to the PAYG plan—its portfolio will differ from the portfolios of institutions through which the voluntary saving is channeled. For example, issues of stocks and bonds may increase at the expense of bank loans. If contributions substitute for payroll taxes, a new market for financial assets (including government paper) is created. If positive externalities are associated with the development of securities markets, a Chilean-style reform may boost economic growth and saving (Holzmann, 1996).

Of basic importance is how the funds are invested. A defined-contributions plan is unlikely to

have an impact on saving different from that of a PAYG plan if the defined-contributions plan's reserves are invested in government securities and the government increases its current expenditure. In such a case, there is no real counterpart to the system's reserves. For Singapore's CPF, the reserves must be invested in government securities, but they are reinvested—mostly abroad. In Chile, the funds of the private pension plans that manage contributors' accounts are invested in a variety of instruments. A large share of the portfolio—about 40 percent in 1994—is invested in government paper, but the government's efforts at fiscal consolidation have not been inhibited by what could have been, in a sense, a captive market.

One important consideration is the treatment given to the government's implicit liability under the old system to those of its former participants who move to the new system. In Chile, the government issued "recognition bonds" (*bonos de reconocimiento*) to these participants. Their value was an approximation of the present value of the expected pension benefits participants had earned while contributing to the old system.[23] In some systems, the records necessary for an accurate determination of the value of the *bono* have not been maintained, so that the formula determining the value is ad hoc. Clearly, the larger the calculated value of the average *bono*, the greater the potential for a wealth effect.

The Chilean reform and, to a much lesser extent, the reform in Peru, caused an increase in the public sector deficit because payroll tax contributions to the state-run system fell when contributors switched to the new, privately administered system. This loss was not fully offset by the contributions made to the new system, because the rate for the new system was less than the combined employer-employee rate for the old. Nonetheless, the impact on aggregate saving of the increase in the deficit was largely offset by the surplus of the new private financial institutions.[24] The rest of the increase was reflected in an increase in take-home pay, which probably increased private sector consumption.[25] Thus, the increase in the deficit—as conventionally measured—overstates the expansionary impact of the reform. Had the contribution rate to the new system been set to equal the combined payroll tax, the surplus of the pension plans would have fully offset the increase in the public sector deficit.[26]

The impact of a Chilean-style reform on national saving depends critically on the method chosen to finance the increase in the deficit that results from the reform. When the deficit is financed through borrowing and the contribution rate of the new system is set equal to the combined payroll tax rate of the old, the disposable income and wealth of the new plan's contributors will not be affected and their saving will not change.[27] The current generation of pensioners will also be unaffected unless the reform includes measures that affect the value of their pension. The government runs an increased deficit, as discussed above, but it is exactly offset by the increased private sector surplus in the form of pension plan surpluses (what were tax payments become involuntary private sector saving). In this case, it is not clear why national saving would be affected.

The result will be different if the government chooses to deal with its increased deficit by adopting a program of fiscal consolidation. The resulting increase in public sector saving should lead to an increase in aggregate saving, because, as discussed, the offset effect of private saving would be less than 100 percent. Thus, a Chilean-style reform cum fiscal consolidation should increase aggregate saving, although it would be the fiscal consolidation, not the pension reform, that increases saving. In fact, one tentative conclusion of research on the Chilean experiment is that the fiscal consolidation of the early to mid-1980s—which was prompted partly by the pension-reform-induced increase in the deficit—contributed to the increase in the national saving rate (Diamond and Valdés-Prieto, 1994; and Holzmann, 1995, 1996). The conversion of the state-run pension system's implicit debt to explicit debt (the *bonos*) may also have helped prompt this consolidation by generating a recognition effect, thereby making consolidation more palatable politically. When the contribution rate is higher than the payroll tax rate, pension reform may increase saving even without fiscal consolidation, although fiscal consolidation should increase saving even more.

---

[23]The *bonos* contribute to the pool of savings that finance the pension plan participants elect upon retirement, but cannot be cashed.

[24]In Peru, the increase in the deficit was smaller than in Chile because of the comparatively small size of the state system and the slower rate of migration to the new system.

[25]In Chile, when contributors switched from the state system to the new plan, their employer no longer had to remit to the government either the employer's or the employee's portion of the payroll tax financing the state scheme. The employee's gross pay rose by the full amount of the payroll tax. Because the rate of contribution to the new plan was set below the (combined) rate of the payroll tax, take-home pay increased.

[26]In this latter case, the reform, while not reducing aggregate saving, could have entailed a financing problem for the public sector if it had not been able to borrow the full amount of the loss in contributions from the pension funds and if other sources had not been available. However, if the pension fund had been lending to the private sector, that lending presumably would have displaced bank or other lending, which could then have been directed to the government. Institutional constraints on the composition of financial institutions' portfolios could nonetheless create problems.

---

[27]If, however, the expected rate of return to contributions under the new system exceeds the expected implicit rate of return under the old, contributors' wealth increases. This will depress their saving.

IV   Private Pension Plans and Saving

The design of public pension plans has the potential to affect the saving rate, as Section III has made clear. The same could be true of private pension plans, and the question arises as to whether the regulatory framework for the private pension industry can be manipulated to increase the saving rate. A related, though distinct, question is whether the private pension industry can replace public schemes without reducing saving or jeopardizing the income security of the elderly.

There may also be scope for raising voluntary (noncontractual) saving. Apart from using macroeconomic policy—for example, by changing the general level of interest rates—governments can conceivably affect the rate of voluntary saving through a number of channels. These include the treatment of saving by the tax system and regulations that affect the perceived soundness of the financial system. Voluntary saving also depends on the extent to which risks to capital and income may be diversified—which in turn depends on the level of development of the financial system—and on the comparative attractiveness of contractual schemes.

There is fairly strong evidence, at least for the United States, that increases in private pension plan saving are not fully offset by declines in voluntary saving (Gale, 1995; and Appendix II). Consequently, there is some reason to believe that an expansion in the patchwork quilt of private pensions could raise the private sector saving rate.

Basic Features of Private Pension Regimes

Because of the tremendous variety in private pension regimes across countries, it is hard to characterize their commonalities and differences. However, the second *tier* of most countries' pension systems (after the public plan) is the occupational, or employer, pension plan. In some countries, plans can be set up on an industrywide basis, as in France. Sometimes they are established with active government involvement—not only in regulation and prudential supervision of investment procedures and policies, but also in basic design issues, such as rates and benefits—as in Israel. The second tier can in some cases be only *semiprivate*, given the government's role as a tacit guarantor of contributors' rights. The coverage of the second tier varies a great deal as well; for example, it is broad in Canada, Switzerland, the United Kingdom, and the United States, and comparatively narrow in Germany.

Private pension plans are typically defined-benefits rather than defined-contributions plans, although the relative importance of the two types does vary across countries. Changes in the tax laws and regulatory frameworks have stimulated increases in the share of defined-contributions plans recently in both the United Kingdom and the United States. The post-retirement indexation of benefits is a rarity, although in most countries where the private regime has broad coverage, the pension takes the form of an annuity.

The legal and regulatory frameworks also vary greatly. A framework normally encompasses the areas of governance, insurance, plan design, and tax status (Box 3).

The quality of pension plan governance has important implications for participants' confidence in their plan and thus for the plans' attractiveness as an alternative to voluntary private saving. So too do insurance requirements, given that company pension plans have been notoriously vulnerable to the company's fortunes. The regulations that apply to plan design, except possibly those governing funding, may not have the same impact on confidence, but can definitely affect the perceived attractiveness of employer pension plans. This is particularly true of the regulations governing vesting and portability. The extent to which private plans are vested or portable varies greatly across countries. Whereas public pension schemes are by definition portable—the plan follows the contributor from job to job, even from job to no job—private pension schemes are typically characterized by little or no portability. Vesting requirements vary substantially, being more strict in some countries than in others.[28]

Funding requirements also vary greatly. In Japan, for example, the rules applying to the annuity plans (tax-qualified pension plans) offered by smaller firms result in less than full funding, because the employers are not required to take account of likely future wage increases in calculating their required reserve. The effective degree of funding is also influenced by the latitude permitted in the selection of actuarial assumptions. Studies of the United States have shown that the actuarial assumptions used for state and local government plans can vary with the financial condition of the employer.[29] The same is likely true of private sector plans.

The tax treatment of private pension regimes is of critical importance for their design, and possibly for their relative size. It is standard practice to exempt contributions from tax, at least up to some ceiling. In this respect, contractual saving is treated more favorably than most forms of purely voluntary saving, al-

though some countries give similarly favorable treatment to contributions made to qualifying individual retirement plans—for example, the individual retirement account (IRA) in the United States, and the registered retirement savings plan (RRSP) in Canada. Some countries also offer at least a limited tax exemption to pension income (Australia), although pensions are generally taxed. In the United States, changes in the tax treatment of defined-contributions plans offered by employers following the 1974 ERISA Act are thought to have contributed to the decline in the share of defined-benefits plans—from 87 percent of all plans in 1975 to 71 percent in 1985.

Regulation and Its Effect on Saving

Clearly, if changes in the regulatory framework are, through their impact on contractual saving, to increase total saving, the increase in saving from that source must not be entirely at the expense of voluntary saving. In a world governed by the LCH, but tempered by some degree of myopia and capital market imperfections, the most obvious way to increase contractual saving is to require higher contribution rates. However, government intervention in the private pension market would then have to go well beyond regulation as such. It would entail two significant problems.

(1) The lack of universal coverage of employer pension plans means that the take-home pay of plan participants would fall relative to that of nonparticipants, which could be perceived as inequitable. Moreover, if plan participants deemed that their real compensation had, on the whole, fallen, the attractiveness of employment at companies or in industries offering pension plans might be reduced. The perceived fall in real compensation would be more likely for contributors to plans with little vesting or portability. If employers were not required to offer pension plans to their employees to begin with, a legal requirement entailing higher contribution rates would simply discourage the plans' creation.

(2) It is not clear how a required contribution rate would work with defined-benefits plans. Presumably, the benefit would be redefined and the replacement ratio would be increased if the required rate exceeded the contribution rate for an existing plan. However, a change in actuarial assumptions could mean that, even with more generous benefits, the contribution rate appropriate for the plan would fall below the rate required by law.

For these and other reasons, the imposition of an obligatory high contribution rate would be problematic for the private pension system. The Chilean system largely avoids these problems, because it is a defined-contributions plan that is compulsory for all

---

[28]For example, U.S. pension legislation (the ERISA Act of 1974) provides that plan participants should in general become vested (i.e., have a right to a pension of some size) after 10 years of participation. In Switzerland, the law requires immediate vesting of employee contributions; employer contributions are partially vested after a few years, but not fully vested until 30 years of plan service. In Japan, there is no legal requirement to vest. In practice, all Japanese plans offer some type of vesting, although it can take 20-30 years to become fully vested. Early leavers are penalized quite heavily.

[29]Hsin and Mitchell (1994).

but the self-employed and because portability is automatic and vesting is 100 percent.[30]

Compulsion not being the strategy of choice, perhaps fiscal incentives are the way to go. There is good evidence that the tax treatment of pensions and other savings vehicles does affect the allocation of saving. It is not clear, however, that it affects total saving (Bovenberg, 1989; Smith, 1990; and Feldstein, 1994). More favorable tax treatment of pension saving is thus likely to be largely—although, the evidence suggests, not fully—financed by a reduction in voluntary saving. Even if it is not, the tax incentives directly reduce public sector saving. Munnell (1992) finds that deferring tax on the accrued benefits of participants in private pension plans in the United States has probably had no impact on national saving. Some recent research on the growth of IRAs and 401(k) plans—two forms of saving favored by the U.S. tax system—has nonetheless concluded that most of it did not come at the expense of other forms of saving (Poterba, Venti, and Wise, 1993).[31]

Another option is measures that affect the riskiness of pension plans and the confidence their contributors have in them. Unfortunately, evidence on the links between the regulatory environment and the coverage of the private pension regime is scanty. A more fundamental point is that, even if pension plans become more attractive (less risky), it is not obvious that the total quantity of saving will grow as a result.

Measures that strengthen the regulatory environment could certainly make contractual saving more attractive relative to voluntary saving, because the effective risk-adjusted return on the former savings vehicle would be increased. However, a large number of studies of the impact of changes in the rate of return to saving on the quantity of saving in the aggregate do not find that the positive impact, if there is one, is large (Savastano, 1995). Moreover, because financial markets do not typically offer life annuities on very favorable terms, the paradoxical effect of measures to promote pension plans could conceivably be a net reduction in private saving. When a company undertakes to provide its employees with life annuities, the amount of money employees save may fall by more than their contributions to the plan if they no longer have to worry about accumulating enough capital to shield themselves from the risk that their returns to investment may be below average and their post-working life longer than normal.[32]

Sound regulatory practices and prudential requirements may entail large welfare gains, promote the development of the private pension industry, and improve financial intermediation. But it is not obvious that they will contribute to an increase in the saving rate. A compulsory defined-contributions system might do so if its contribution rate is high enough, although such a system would have to be properly integrated with existing public and private schemes, which it might at least partially replace.

---

[30]A Chilean-style plan need not be optional for the self-employed, although the regulatory and administrative requirements of a defined-contributions plan that is compulsory for all are much more substantial than those for one confined to wage and salary earners.

[31]The increase in saving induced by tax incentives or reforms could have feedback effects on interest rates that could depress saving.

[32]People who are risk averse will seek to accumulate a stock of savings whose value will exceed the expected present value of the post-retirement consumption stream they want to finance, at least when the present value is calculated at a rate of interest close to the market rate. By the same token, shortsighted people—those who, were they not members of a company pension plan, would not save enough—will have their saving rate increased. See Auerbach and Kotlikoff (1995) for a discussion of this issue.

Appendix I   Pension Arrangements in an Overlapping-Generations Model

This appendix uses an overlapping-generations model to look at the impact of introducing funded and unfunded social security systems, and of replacing an unfunded system with a funded one. The analysis follows closely the overlapping-generations model presented in chapter 3 of Blanchard and Fischer (1989) and illustrates the main findings of the text of this paper: that the introduction of a fully funded pension scheme should have no impact on the level of private savings unless the mandatory contribution rate is very high; that the introduction of an unfunded PAYG scheme will tend to decrease private saving; and that the replacement of an existing PAYG scheme with a fully funded scheme will not typically increase saving unless it is accompanied by a fiscal consolidation.

The Model

The economy consists of individuals and firms. Individuals live for two periods and consume $c_{1,t}$ in period t and $c_{2,t+1}$ in period $t + 1$. An individual's lifetime utility is given by

$$u(c_{1,t}) + (1 + \theta)^{-1} u(c_{2,t+1}),$$

where $\theta > 0$, $u' > 0$, and $u'' < 0$. Individuals work only in the first period of their lives, supplying labor inelastically and earning a wage w_t. They consume part of their labor income and save the rest, investing their savings to finance their second-period consumption.

The saving of the young in period t generates the capital stock that is used in period $t + 1$ in combination with the labor supplied by the young generation in that period. The number of individuals born at time t and working in that period is N_t. Population growth is given exogenously at rate n.

Firms behave competitively and produce output using the constant-returns-to-scale production function $Y = F(K, N)$. Output per worker is given by the production function $y = f(k)$, where k is the capital-labor ratio. Assume the production function satisfies the Inada conditions[33] and that firms take the wage

rate and the rental price of capital, r_t, as given when maximizing profits.

The maximization problem for the individuals is given as

$$\max u(c_{1,t}) + (1 + \theta)^{-1} u(c_{2,t+1}),$$

subject to

$$c_{1,t} + s_t = w_t$$

and

$$c_{2,t+1} \leq s_t (1 + r_{t+1}).$$

(In the second period, individuals consume both their savings and the interest income earned by them.) The first-order condition for a maximum is

$$u'(w_t - s_t) - (1 + \theta)^{-1} \cdot (1 + r_{t+1})u'[s_t(1 + r_{t+1})] = 0, \qquad (1)$$

which implies a savings function

$$s_t = s(w_t, r_{t+1}), \qquad (2)$$

where $0 < s_w < 1$ and the sign of s_r is ambiguous because of offsetting income and substitution effects.[34]

The maximization problem for firms yields the familiar first-order conditions

$$f(k_t) - k_t f'(k_t) = w_t$$

and

$$f'(k_t) = r_t. \qquad (3)$$

Finally, goods-market equilibrium requires that the demand for and the supply of goods be equal or, equivalently, that savings equal investment. In other words, the stock of capital at $t + 1$ must equal the savings of the young generation at t:

$$(1 + n)k_{t+1} = s(w_t, r_{t+1}). \qquad (4)$$

---

[33]That is, $f' > 0$, $f'' < 0$, $\lim_{k \to 0} f' = \infty$ and $\lim_{k \to \infty} f' = 0$.

[34]A higher interest rate means that each additional unit of current-period saving will allow a greater increase in second-period consumption than was previously the case. At the margin, that will tend to increase savings (the substitution effect). At the same time, the higher interest rate increases the level of second-period consumption that can be financed from the existing stock of first-period savings, which tends to decrease the level of saving (the income effect).

These first-order conditions define the equilibrium. Blanchard and Fischer (1989) show that under certain restrictions, the equilibrium will be a stable one.[35]

Funded Social Security

In a fully funded system, the government (or, more generally, the pension fund) in period t collects contributions of d_t from the young and invests the proceeds in the capital stock. It also pays benefits of $b_t = (1 + r_t)d_{t-1}$ to the old, whose contribution was invested in period $t - 1$. Equations (1) and (4) thus become

$$u'[w_t - (s_t + d_t)] - (1 + \theta)^{-1}$$
$$\cdot (1 + r_{t+1})u'[(s_t + d_t)(1 + r_{t+1})] = 0 \qquad (5)$$

and

$$s_t + d_t = (1 + n)k_{t+1}. \qquad (6)$$

Comparing equations (1) and (4) with equations (5) and (6), it is clear that if k_t solves the former set, it also solves the latter, as long as $d_t < (1 + n) k_{t+1}$. That is, as long as the required contribution under the fully funded scheme does not exceed the level of voluntary saving that would exist without the pension scheme, the introduction of a fully funded scheme does not affect the level of private saving. Individuals earn the same return on pension savings as on any other form of savings and are therefore indifferent between the allocation of s and d. They simply adjust their voluntary saving s to take into account any mandatory savings d.

Unfunded System

In an unfunded system, first-period income still falls by d_t and second-period income still increases by b_t, but now the benefit paid in period t is equal to the contribution paid in during that same period; that is, $b_t = (1 + n)d_t$. In other words, if each worker's contribution to the pension fund is constant over time (as it is in the steady state in this model), the return on pension contributions is only n rather than r.

Under these circumstances, equations (1) and (4) become

$$u'[w_t - (s_t + d_t)] - (1 + \theta)^{-1}$$
$$\cdot (1 + r_{t+1})u'[s_t(1 + r_{t+1}) + d_{t+1}(1 + n)] = 0 \quad (7)$$

and

$$s_t = (1 + n)k_{t+1}. \qquad (8)$$

It is straightforward to show that both the saving rate and the per capita stock of capital are decreasing functions of the required contribution rate. First, differentiating equation (7) with respect to the contribution rate (assuming that $d_t = d_{t+1}$) yields

$$\frac{\partial s_t}{\partial d_t} = -\frac{u_1'' + (1 - \theta)^{-1}(1 + r)(1 + n)u_2''}{u_1''(1 - \theta)^{-1}(1 + r)^2 u_2''},$$

which is unambiguously negative, meaning that private saving falls when an unfunded system is introduced. Differentiation of equation (8) through the implicit function rule yields

$$\frac{\partial k_{t+1}}{\partial d_t} = \frac{\partial s_t / \partial d_t}{1 + n - s_r f''},$$

which is also negative.[36] Thus, both private saving and the stock of capital fall when an unfunded pension scheme is introduced.

Replacing an Unfunded with a Funded System

Now suppose that an unfunded system is replaced by a fully funded one. For the current generation of retirees, the government has an obligation that it finances by borrowing from the young generation at the market interest rate.

Because the value of the obligation owed to retirees is unaffected by the change, the amount the government borrows per worker, z_t, must be the same as the amount it would have collected from each worker under the old PAYG system, d_t. Therefore, equations (1) and (4) become

$$u'[w_t - (s_t + z_t)] - (1 + \theta)^{-1}$$
$$\cdot (1 + r_{t+1})u'[(s_t + z_t)(1 + r_{t+1})] = 0 \qquad (9)$$

and

$$s_t = (1 + n)k_{t+1}. \qquad (10)$$

Assuming, as before, that $d_t = d_{t+1}$, equations (7) and (8) are identical to equations (9) and (10) except that the portion of savings going to finance the retirement consumption of the currently old earns a return of r_{t+1} rather than n. This increase in the inframarginal rate will generate a pure income effect that will tend to discourage current-period saving. Thus, the transition from a PAYG to a fully funded system

---

[35]The main restriction is that at the equilibrium per capita stock of capital k^*,

$$\left| \frac{dk_{t+1}}{dk_t} \right| = \left| \frac{-s_w k^* f''(k^*)}{1 + n - s_r f''(k^*)} \right| < 1 .$$

[36]To obtain the denominator, note that $\partial s / \partial k = (\partial s / \partial r) \times (\partial r / \partial k)$, and that $r = f'(k)$.

generates an immediate income effect that lowers private saving.

Assuming that no fiscal consolidation accompanies the change in pension systems, the government will need to continue refloating its debt. Thus, to repay in period $t + 1$ the funds it borrowed in period t, the government will need to borrow $z_{t+1} = z_t(1 + r_{t+1})/(1 + n)$ from each worker in period $t + 1$. The first-order conditions for a worker in period $t + 1$ therefore become

$$u'[w_{t+1} - (s_{t+1} + z_{t+1})]$$
$$= (1 + \theta)^{-1}(1 + r_{t+2}) + z_{t+1})(1 + r_{t+2})] \qquad (11)$$

and

$$s_{t+1} = (1 + n)k_{t+2}. \qquad (12)$$

If, as is commonly assumed, $r > n$, then the per worker stock of debt increases in each period, leading (in partial equilibrium) to a decrease in savings for capital accumulation and a lower capital stock. From equation (11), increases in z are fully offset by decreases in s (given that individuals are indifferent between buying government debt and investing in capital) until voluntary savings are exhausted. However, this is a partial equilibrium result in that it treats the interest rate as given. Clearly, as the stock of capital

falls, the rate of interest will rise and labor income will fall, both of which will influence the level of saving. To move to general equilibrium, we can differentiate equation (12) with respect to z_{t+1} to show

$$\frac{dk_{t+2}}{dz_{t+1}} = \frac{\partial s_{t+1} / \partial d_{t+1}}{1 + n - s_r f''(k_{t+2})},$$

where s_r is the derivative of savings with respect to the interest rate. Given that $f'' < 0$, if s_r is nonnegative, then the effect of an increase in government borrowing per worker is to unambiguously decrease the stock of capital in general equilibrium.

Notice also that the path of z_t is unsustainable over time, because it grows at the rate of $(1 + r)/(1 + n)$. Financing the transition with debt leads to spiraling government deficits, even though the underlying primary fiscal balance is constant. Although the decline in the capital stock will lead to an increase in the interest rate and generate additional savings, the explosive path of z_t will eventually exhaust output. Accordingly, some adjustment in the primary fiscal balance will be required to ensure stability in the model. It may be in this indirect sense that the switch from a PAYG to a fully funded scheme encourages saving.

Appendix II   Notes on the Empirical Literature on Pensions and Saving

Given the theoretical ambiguity of the precise relationship between pensions and saving, the various statistical techniques that have been used to analyze it, and the diversity in actual pension systems and in the underlying socioeconomic and demographic profiles of different countries at different times, it is not surprising to find a wide range of results in the empirical literature. In general, the evidence is rather weak, although it suggests that public pension systems have a small negative effect (a positive effect, however, has been found in a few countries) on aggregate saving rates and that private retirement schemes have a more clearly positive effect on saving. First, this appendix reviews the literature on public pensions, with a special emphasis on a group of studies that rely on the construction of a social security wealth variable. Then, it discusses the results concerning private retirement schemes.

Some Empirical Findings on Public Pensions

Studies of the United States

Experience with the public pension system of the *United States* has been studied extensively. However, the results of this effort have not been conclusive. Cross-sectional studies tend to find considerable substitution between private wealth and social security wealth (SSW), but the offset is generally less than dollar for dollar: in several studies offsets were found to range from 39 cents to 69 cents per dollar of SSW.[37] Working with total (public and private) pension wealth, Gale (1995) attempts to control for a number of factors that may bias the estimated offset toward zero and succeeds in obtaining offset estimates as high as 82 cents per dollar. However, the author recognizes possible sample bias away from zero as well and concludes that extending pension coverage may well increase saving because this would increase involuntary saving by finan-

cially naive or liquidity-constrained individuals who would not engage in offsetting behavior.

Feldstein (1974) was the first researcher to incorporate the effect of pensions into an estimable version of the life-cycle model for the United States through an SSW variable. Under the LCH, individuals make consumption decisions on the basis of their total human and nonhuman wealth. Therefore, the total (current and future) anticipated financial flows, appropriately discounted, expected to be derived from participation in a pension plan must be taken into account to explain current consumption and saving. Using aggregate data, Feldstein estimates a model of the following form:

$$C_t = a + b\, Y_t + c\, W_{t-1} + d\, SSW_t.$$

This model makes current consumption depend on contemporaneous disposable income Y, accumulated financial and real wealth W, and anticipated SSW. SSW is the present value of the expected retirement benefits payable to those currently at work or currently retired, from the present time onward. It can be calculated net or gross of future contributions to the social security system.

This type of formulation has been used extensively, and results can vary widely according to how the SSW series is constructed. The basic building block is the social security wealth of a representative individual from a well-defined group (e.g., active worker of a certain sex, age, and marital status; current retiree of a certain sex, age, and marital status; spouse and children eligible for survivor benefits). The SSW variable is constructed by first summing the individuals in each category, and then summing over the categories.

A useful example is that of an unmarried worker of age A in year t who is eligible to retire with a full pension at age 65 without ever having married. With some probability, this individual will live to see his sixty-fifth birthday, and thus $65 - A$ years from year t, in year $t + 65 - A$, he will begin collecting retirement benefits. In his first year as a retiree, he will collect B_{t+65-A}, and with some probability, he will survive another year to collect B_{t+66-A}, and so forth. Then, as of his sixty-fifth birthday, it is assumed that he can

---

[37]Munnell (1985) and Gale (1995) survey some of these studies.

compute the present value of the total stream of pension payments he will henceforth receive, discounting them year by year at some appropriate rate and by the probability that he will not live to receive the payments. This is the expected present value of his pension at the time of retirement. In year t, when the worker is still A years old, he is assumed to be able to foresee and estimate this value, and to discount it to time t, taking into account the probability of his not reaching retirement age. This is his gross social security wealth in year t. To arrive at a net measure of SSW, the present value of the contributions the worker will pay between the years t and $t + 65 - A$ is computed and then subtracted from gross SSW. For other categories of covered individuals, the computations are analogous.

This description of the method for computing SSW has left many details unresolved: What is the appropriate discount factor? What measure of benefits in, say, 1970, B_{70}, do we use when constructing a 45-year-old individual's SSW 20 years earlier?[38] In particular, how do we deal with changes in the rules for computing benefits that have taken place? Do we assume that people could anticipate these changes, and if so, since when? How do we deal with the possibility of early or late retirement? How do we incorporate those currently unemployed who may be rehired later and the possibility that those currently at work may face unemployment at some future time? How do we take into account the possibility that a worker, unmarried at some point, may have expected to marry later and have children who might eventually collect survivor benefits? We could resolve some of these issues, at least for the average member of each category, if we had enough data at our disposal, but at the cost of making estimation impractical.[39] For example, we could probably deal with changes in marital status or retirement at ages other than 65, but other issues have no "best" answer, and the choices may crucially affect the results.[40]

The most important and controversial issue relates to the way people form expectations about the level of future benefits. Feldstein (1974) assumes that people expect the average replacement ratio to be constant, which leads him to set expected benefits for every year at 41 percent of disposable income per head (its mean value in the sample period 1947–71). Feldstein also assumes that people expect disposable income to grow at 2 percent a year in real terms. He finds that the marginal propensity to consume pension wealth is higher than the propensity to consume financial and real wealth, something he ascribes to the higher concentration in the distribution of the latter across households. He concludes that, in the absence of social security, private saving would have been between 40 percent and 50 percent higher than it was at the time of his study. He reaches similar conclusions in later versions of his work (Feldstein, 1982 and 1995); in his most recent exercise, Feldstein (1995) estimates that the social security program reduces private saving by close to 60 percent.

However, different assumptions can be made to compute future benefits. Leimer and Lesnoy (1982) start with the same primitive data as Feldstein (1974), but do more refined actuarial work on the demographic and labor market assumptions required to construct SSW. They then try different approaches to computating benefits: perfect foresight (benefits are anticipated exactly), myopia (current levels are expected to remain unchanged in real terms), and constant average replacement rates. In most cases, their results indicate that pensions have no statistically discernible influence on saving—the exception is the model with the Feldstein-type of assumption. They then try estimating over different periods, and the results turn out to be highly sensitive to even small changes in, for example, the starting year of the sample.

Other studies have been inspired by the SSW approach. Using the SSW variable constructed by Leimer and Lesnoy (1982), Burkhauser and Turner (1982) find that one effect of social security in the United States has been to increase the work week by two or three hours among "prime-aged" men. Exclusion of this effect from the saving regressions discussed above will tend to produce results that exaggerate the negative effect of pensions on saving.

Using a somewhat different approach, Leimer and Richardson (1992) study the effect of social security on saving and on economic efficiency by estimating a model that incorporates the benefits from reducing longevity risk (the risk that an old person may outlast his savings). They conclude that social security does reduce voluntary saving by a significant amount, but still less than dollar for dollar. In fact, they must reject extreme life-cycle and Ricardian versions of their consumption equations, because they find negative effects on saving through life-cycle channels, but also some offsets to these effects through private transfers. Perhaps more important, their findings suggest that over one-half of saving reductions attributable to social security represent efficiency gains because pensions satisfy a need that imperfect annuities markets do not fully meet.

---

[38]In other words, what benefits did a 45-year-old worker think, in 1950, that he would receive as a retiree in 1970?

[39]Not to mention the fact that the more complex the method for constructing SSW, the more prone to error the actual construction will be.

[40]See Auerbach and Kotlikoff (1983) for a discussion of how different assumptions, such as the choice of the sample period to analyze, can determine the results of this type of research.

Studies of Other Countries

The impact on saving of pension systems in other countries has received less intense scrutiny, but some analyses are available. In *Italy*, an *SSW* series has been constructed to study the decline in saving over recent years that has coincided with marked growth in the ratio of pension expenditure to GDP (Rossi and Visco, 1992). The study assumes a myopic formation of expectations about future benefits and finds that the social security system reduced private saving by about one-third in 1990. It also states that, while about one-fourth of the fall in private saving between the 1960s and the 1980s can be attributed to rising *SSW*, virtually all of the fall in private saving during the 1980s is attributable to that source.

Another study of the Italian experience also finds that SSW partially substitutes for other assets, but the offset effect is in the range of 10–20 percent (Jappelli, 1995).[41] The Italian pension system is one of the most generous among OECD countries; given the levels of contributions, current benefits are estimated to be at least 21 percent higher than they would be if the system were funded.[42]

Japan's social security system, introduced in 1942, underwent significant changes in 1965 and 1973 that offer an opportunity to study the effects of successive and drastic increases in the coverage and generosity of pensions. Yamada and Yamada (1988) and Yamada, Yamada, and Liu (1990) study time-series data for Japan following the extended life-cycle model proposed by Feldstein (1974), but attempt to separate more carefully the impact of pensions on private saving into a negative "benefit" effect and a positive "retirement" effect. The 1988 study finds that the benefit effect is about ten times larger than the retirement effect in Japan, and that, on balance, saving was depressed by 68 percent as a result of growth in pension wealth during 1970–80.

Another study (Yamada, Yamada, and Liu, 1992) also tries to disentangle the retirement and benefit effects, using a system of equations with personal saving rates and labor force participation as endogenous variables. It estimates that the real increase in social security wealth since 1960 caused personal saving to be reduced by 34–38 percent in 1980. The findings are robust to the choice of social security variable (social security contributions, gross or net SSW), and the authors conclude that social security does depress savings in Japan. An earlier paper by Yamada, Yamada, and Liu (1990) focuses on the effects of the institutional changes of 1965 and 1973,

which increased benefits and relaxed eligibility criteria. It finds that each of these reforms magnified the depressing net effect of social security on private saving.

A study of *Canada* (Denny and Rea, 1979), however, finds that the saving rate is higher than it was prior to the introduction of the Canada Pension Plan in 1966, instead of lower by 5.2 percentage points as it should be under the dollar-for-dollar replacement hypothesis. These authors suggest that the induced-retirement effect may be responsible for this result. A government study in Ontario covering 1951–75[43] finds a negative but statistically insignificant direct effect of benefits on saving ratios, a negative and significant direct effect of coverage, and an insignificant but positive retirement effect. However, retirement itself is significantly increased by pension coverage and benefits. On the whole, the latter study finds that the overall impact of pensions on saving was positive but statistically insignificant. It concludes that the saving rate may have increased by up to 3.8 percentage points as a result of the pension plan, but also that as the proportion of people who retire reaches a plateau, the negative benefit effects will become preponderant.

One survey of the *United Kingdom* (Barros, 1979) focuses on the natural experiment created by the social security reforms undertaken there during the 1970s. It reports that studies have tended to find small negative, or even positive, effects of pensions on other forms of personal saving. While inconclusive, these studies are interpreted as lending support to the hypothesis that pensions induce retirement, not just by making it more affordable (feasible), but also by making people aware that they should make provisions toward their old age (the "recognition effect"). At any rate, no evidence is presented to the effect that pensions depress saving. Elsewhere, impressionistic arguments have been advanced to the effect that private savings growth has been hampered by the presence of social security (Seldon, 1994).

A study of *France* (Oudet, 1979), while using very rough data and simple methods, finds that pensions do not depress saving. The study suggests that, in France, (1) wealth is largely held in real estate, for which pensions are poor substitutes; (2) wealth and savings are quite concentrated; and (3) old people do not run down their financial wealth to a significant extent. These findings would point to a system of private intergenerational transfers through which some of the negative "benefit effect" can be undone (40 percent of net worth in France as of the mid-1970s was estimated to be the result of inheritance).

---

[41]This study controls for desired retirement age, which should in principle result in more accurate estimates of SSW.

[42]See Canziani and Demekas (1995).

[43]Reported also in Denny and Rea (1979).

In addition, the recognition effect is mentioned again as a contribution made by pension systems to promote saving.

A study of *Germany* (Blum and Gaudry, 1987) uses a cross-sectional approach in which household saving is related to gross income, taxes, household composition, and contributions to the public pension system. Its main finding is that the sign on the social security variable is not robust to changes in the regression equation's functional form.

A study of *Belgium* (Perelman and Pestieau, 1984) adopts an approach similar to Feldstein's, with results that are consistent with the Feldstein hypothesis; moreover, the results are robust with respect to changes in the specification of the regression equation.

In *Sweden*, where a partially funded system has been in place since 1960, studies suggest that voluntary saving may have fallen as a result of the operation of the public pension scheme. The drop in the household saving ratio is estimated at between 1.5 percentage points and 4.0 percentage points in different studies.[44] However, the growth of the general pension fund during 1960–80 represents a saving of between 2 percent and 4.5 percent of GDP. On balance, therefore, aggregate saving does not seem to have been affected by the pension scheme and may even have increased slightly.

Voluntary saving has been declining as a proportion of total income in the *Netherlands* for over three decades. Draper (1994) argues that an important factor in this development has been the generosity of pensions. The model used to generate this result rests on the idea that people may make medium-term decisions on consumption and asset accumulation, because lifelong planning may be impossible or too onerous in view of the uncertainty surrounding income flows. The results indicate that a unit decrease in pension rights will lead to an offsetting increase in financial wealth of about 40 percent.

Shome and Saito (1980) explore the economic impact of social security systems in five Asian countries: *India, Malaysia, Philippines, Singapore,* and *Sri Lanka*. In each of these countries, saving through social security schemes (contributions to funded schemes and surpluses of PAYG schemes[45]) comprised between 20 percent and 45 percent of gross household financial saving during the 1970s. The importance of social security would lead one to expect a crowding out of "noncompulsory saving."

The authors run simple regressions to test this conjecture and find that pension saving does not significantly reduce voluntary saving; if anything, it seems to increase it in some cases (India, Singapore, and Sri Lanka). In fact, in all five countries, voluntary and compulsory saving seem to follow parallel and usually upward trends. The authors suggest that, except in Singapore, urbanization may be one cause underlying the increases in both types of saving. As more workers migrate to cities, they take jobs in the formal economy, which makes them subject to social security contributions; at the same time, they face the need to build savings to substitute for the more traditional safety nets provided by the networks of transfers left behind in rural areas.

A study of prereform *Chile* (Wallich, 1981) tries to estimate the benefit and retirement effects of the old PAYG social security scheme, loosely following the extended life-cycle model. The main result is that, although a clear retirement effect can be identified, the benefit effect is consistently positive and statistically significant under different model specifications. On balance, the pension scheme in Chile stimulates voluntary saving. This study offers numerous possible explanations for the absence of an offsetting effect on private saving, among them the weak credibility of the scheme and problems with the data.

A review of econometric studies of the effects of compulsory saving on national saving in Malaysia reports that most of the studies cited find that the presence of the compulsory defined-contributions plan reduces national saving (Chang, 1995). The reason, apparently, is that the compulsory saving plans do not induce households to increase their saving, but simply lead them to reduce their discretionary saving by an offsetting amount. However, the employer contribution redistributes income from the high-saving corporate sector to the low-saving household sector, leading to a decline in aggregate private saving. Public saving may also decline as a result of the compulsory saving plan, with the presence of ready credit from the Employees' Provident Fund (which must invest 50 percent of its assets in government securities, down from 70 percent earlier) inducing the government to spend more than it otherwise might.

Cross-Sectional or Panel Approaches

From a different methodological perspective, Feldstein (1977) attempts to explain variations in saving rates across countries by estimating an extended life-cycle model for a cross section of 15 countries with well-established social security systems. He concludes that pension systems reduce national saving rates and thus endanger the

---

[44]See Palmer (1988) for a summary of the findings of these studies and a description of Sweden's pension system.

[45]Shome and Saito (1980) explain that defined-benefits plans mobilize at least as much savings as funded systems in these countries, largely as a consequence of the immaturity of the schemes.

prospects for capital accumulation. In particular, he notes that the benefit effect reduces the saving rate by over 4 percentage points in the United States. On average for the sample, the net impact of the benefit (negative) and retirement (positive) effects is to reduce the saving rate by 1.5 percentage points.

Barro and MacDonald (1979) use a pooled cross-sectional time-series sample of data on 16 Western industrial countries during 1951–60 to test a model of consumer spending. They find that their results depend strongly on whether the model is estimated with a single intercept term, or if individual country intercepts are introduced. Using a common intercept, the social security variable (total payments for old-age, survivors' and disability programs, divided by the number of individuals aged 65 and over, as a share of per capita income) has a significant, negative effect on consumption. However, when individual country intercepts are used, the results indicate that social security has a significant, positive effect on consumption. (In addition, the assumption of a common intercept is rejected at the 1 percent level.) One implication of these results is that time-series properties of the data set (captured by the individual intercept model) imply a negative relationship between saving and social security, while the cross-sectional properties, more fully captured in the common intercept specification, imply a positive one. A second implication is that the results of cross-sectional studies like this one are extremely sensitive to model specification.

Kopits and Gotur (1980) adopt a cross-sectional approach, but examine data from both industrial and developing countries. (Specifically, they look at averaged data covering 1969–71 for 14 industrial and 40 developing countries.) They estimate a separate labor force participation function for individuals aged 65 and over, and include old-age pensions, old-age lump-sum payments, other social security transfers, and loans from social security funds as separate variables, rather than lumping all social security payments into a single variable. In addition, they use private household saving, rather than total private saving, as their dependent variable. For industrial countries, they find that increases in social security pensions tend to increase household saving (as do increases in social security tax rates), while increases in other social security benefits tend to reduce saving. The implication is that the indirect effect of higher social security pensions on saving that operates through labor force participation rates (they find that the presence of social security payments—in the form of pensions or lump-sum payments—reduces labor force participation rates for those over 65) outweighs the direct wealth effect. Social security pensions also tend to reduce labor force participation in developing countries, but the overall im-

pact of pensions on saving in these countries is close to zero, because the direct and indirect effects almost cancel each other out. As in industrial countries, other forms of social security benefits tend to reduce saving.

Modigliani and Sterling (1983) examine a cross section of 21 OECD countries using period averages covering 1960–70, modeling private saving and participation rates of older workers as functions of—among other variables—replacement ratios for social security systems. They find that their results are extremely sensitive to the specification of the variables other than social security included in the study and to the presence of extreme observations within the sample. In addition, they gather data on replacement ratios from two different sources (neither of which covers all countries in the sample) and find that their results depend on which replacement ratios are used.[46] They find that social security has a small, negative direct effect on private saving, but a large, negative effect on participation rates. The net effect of these two forces on savings is insignificant, meaning that the direct and indirect effects largely cancel each other out.

Koskela and Viren (1986) also follow a cross-sectional approach, using a model with pooled cross-country data under a variety of assumptions about the error term. The data consist of annual observations for the period 1960–77 drawn from 16 OECD countries. The model regresses the saving-to-GDP ratio on country dummies, a number of macroeconomic and demographic controls, and the ratio of social security benefits per retiree to per capita GDP. The authors cannot reject the null of a zero coefficient on the social security variable. They also run separate regressions for each country with a reduced number of regressors. These tend to yield the same result; only in Portugal and Sweden are significant and negative coefficients found. The authors conclude, as they did in an earlier study (Koskela and Viren, 1983) that used essentially the same model, that social security has no effect on household saving.

In summary, several cross-sectional studies have found a negative direct effect of social security on saving, but they have also often found that social security induces earlier retirement, which indirectly leads to higher saving. Overall, the two effects appear to cancel each other out, meaning that social security has no net impact on saving. These studies have also demonstrated that results are extremely sensitive to the specifications researchers choose to employ.

---

[46]They also find that among countries covered by both sources, the replacement rates differ significantly for individual countries.

What may be concluded from this survey? Clearly, different studies have come to widely varying conclusions about the impact of social security on saving. A number of studies—particularly those of the United States—tend to find some, but less than full, offset of public pension saving through reduced private saving. Others conclude that pension schemes may actually increase private saving. To this extent, offering a general conclusion—one that applies across countries—on the impact of pensions on saving is not possible.

Occupational Pensions and Saving: Some Empirical Results

As is often the case, economic theory is considerably better at identifying the various forces through which participation in occupational pension programs influences individuals' saving decisions than it is at providing insight into the likely magnitudes, and hence overall effect, of these forces.

To resolve this theoretical ambiguity, a number of economists have undertaken empirical studies of the extent to which participation in pension plans affects aggregate saving. The simplest estimating equation for such a study would take the form

$$W = a'z + bP + e,$$

where W is nonpension wealth or savings, z is a vector of explanatory (usually demographic) variables, P is a scalar measuring pension wealth, e is an error term, and $[a', b]$ is a vector of coefficients to be estimated. If $b = -1$, then pension savings fully offset other savings, and total savings, $W + P$, are unaffected by increases in pension wealth. If $b > -1$, then the offset is less than full (and if $b > 0$, the offset is negative), and increases in pension wealth would lead to increases in aggregate wealth.[47]

Cagan (1965), in an early study, finds that households with pensions tend to have higher nonpension savings than households that are not covered by pension plans, but he fails to control for any demographic variables that might also affect saving behavior. When Munnell (1974) controls for age, education, income, and other factors, she finds a negative impact of pension saving on other saving, but the effect is not statistically significant. In a subsequent paper, she adds controls for the desire to leave an inheritance, expected retirement age, and life expectancy—high values of these variables would tend

to increase saving—and finds that about 62 percent of pension wealth is offset by reductions in other savings (Munnell, 1976). However, Kotlikoff (1979) uses the same data set and finds no significant effect of pension coverage on wealth or saving. Blinder, Gordon, and Wise (1980) find a positive but insignificant effect of private pension wealth on other wealth, while Waters (1981) looks at Canadian data and finds that, on average, homeowners reduce their nonpension wealth by about 50 cents for every dollar they contribute to their pension plans. Diamond and Hausman (1984) find that, while more generous annual pension benefits induce earlier retirement, they have little direct effect on saving rates or wealth.

Dicks-Mireaux and King (1984) use Canadian data to examine the impact of pension wealth on the ratio of private wealth to permanent income. They find that the offset for pension wealth is between 27 percent and 51 percent, meaning that each increase of a dollar in pension wealth leads to a reduction of between 27 cents and 51 cents in nonpension wealth (or to an increase of 49 cents to 73 cents in total wealth). Pitelis (1985) examines postwar U.K. data and finds no evidence of an offset of nonpension saving from contributions to pension funds or life insurance. Hubbard (1986) uses data on American households and finds that the average offset is 16 percent (which is much lower than the offset he finds for social security), while Avery, Elliehausen, and Gustafson (1986) find (using a sample of American households headed by persons aged 50 and over) that the offset is 66 percent when a broad measure of nonpension wealth is used, but only 11 percent when nonpension wealth includes only liquid assets. Venti and Wise (1986) examine the likely impact of raising the ceiling on contributions to IRAs in the United States and find that on average, only about 10–20 percent of increased IRA contributions come at the expense of holdings of other financial assets, with 45–55 percent of that from reduced consumption and about 35 percent from lower taxes. Bernheim and Scholz (1993) find that pension coverage reduces nonpension wealth for households headed by college graduates but not for others. Poterba, Venti, and Wise (1993) find that saving in IRAs and 401(k) plans has little impact on other forms of saving, while Venti and Wise (1996) find very little (or even negative) offset from pension wealth.

Not surprisingly, these empirical studies have produced a wide variety of results. In some, the offset is as large as 66 percent, while in others it is close to zero, and in still others it is negative. However, none of the studies finds an offset of 100 percent, and thus all the studies imply that increases in occupational or private pension saving will induce increases in aggregate saving. Whether an increase of a dollar in

---

[47]Given that $W = a'z + bP + e$, it is clear that $W + P = a'z + (1 + b)P + e$. Therefore, if $b = -1$, total wealth, $W + P$, is independent of P. If $b > -1$, then total wealth is increasing in P, while if $b < -1$, then total wealth is decreasing in P.

pension saving leads to an increase of 33 cents, a dollar, or more than a dollar in aggregate saving remains an open question. However, none of the studies supports the contention that increases in pension saving have no impact on the level of aggregate saving. From a public policy perspective, the implication is that an expansion of private pension systems could lead to a significant increase in private saving. In addition, to the extent that wealthier households are more likely than poorer ones to offset higher pension saving with reduced nonpension saving, an expansion of private pension programs could have positive social implications by redistributing wealth.

As Gale (1995) notes, a number of econometric problems—mostly related to omitted variables or measurement errors—can arise in estimating the effects of private pensions on aggregate saving and can bias the results. For example, if saving is calculated from cash earnings rather than from total compensation (including deferred compensation), the offset will tend to be underestimated because it will not take into account the income effect arising from higher future compensation.[48] Omitting variables for

life expectancy, retirement age, and current age (as some studies have done), or ignoring the fact that employment choices are endogenous and that people with high propensities to save may self-select into jobs that offer pensions, may also introduce a bias that understates the extent of the offset. Having corrected for many of these factors, Gale obtains an estimated offset of 82 percent in one exercise and 39 percent in another. Although these estimates are substantially larger than those from most of the studies cited above, they are still less than 100 percent. Moreover, because Gale's sample is wealthier than average, and because the degree of offset tends to increase with wealth, his results may overstate the extent of the offset for the population as a whole. In any case, the bulk of the available econometric evidence does not reject the view that nonpension wealth is insensitive to private pension wealth, implying that any offset of nonpension saving arising from increases in pension saving is small.

---

[48]Consider two individuals, each of whom earns a cash wage of 100 in period 1 and lives off of his savings and retirement income in period 2. The first individual will receive a pension of 10 in period 2, while the second individual will receive no retirement income. If each smooths his consumption perfectly over the two periods, the first individual will consume 55 in period 1 and enter period 2 with 45 in savings, while the second will consume 50 in period 1 and enter period 2 with 50 in savings. Thus, the increase of 10 in pension wealth appears to have led to a decline of 5 in nonpension wealth, implying an offset of 50 percent. However, the true offset is 100 percent, because if the first individual had received his true income of 110 in cash he would have entered period 2 with 55 in savings rather than the 45 he actually began with.

Appendix III   Brief Notes on the Pension Regimes of Selected Countries

Private Plans in Selected Industrial Countries

Japan

Private retirement plans in Japan are either lump-sum severance payment plans or pension plans that provide annuity benefits. Ninety percent of all firms offer one or both types of retirement plans, and virtually all firms with more than 300 employees offer some type of retirement plan for their regular workers. Even among firms with only 30–99 workers, more than 85 percent offer a retirement plan. Traditionally, most firms have offered lump-sum retirement payments, but annuities have become increasingly popular. Between 1975 and 1985, the percentage of firms offering only lump-sum severance payments fell from 67 percent to 52 percent. The trend toward annuities is even stronger in larger firms.

Lump-Sum Plans

Among firms offering lump-sum severance packages, payments are available regardless of the cause of a worker's departure, although typically the value of the payment is sharply reduced when departure is voluntary, with the extent of the reduction depending on the worker's length of service. Workers become eligible for some form of lump-sum severance payment after two to three years of service. The value of the lump-sum benefit at retirement is usually a function of years of service, typically one month of final salary for each year of service. In 1988, the average benefit paid to male college graduates retiring at age 60 was equal to about 3.5 years of annual salary.

Employers with lump-sum retirement benefits can establish a reserve fund in a public (external) financial institution from which to pay them. Alternatively, they may establish a book reserve within their own firm. These book reserves are an important source of capital for many firms and effectively make paying lump-sum severance benefits contingent on the firm's financial performance. For funds invested within the firm, employers receive a tax de-

duction equal to the lesser of 40 percent of the amount that would be payable if all workers voluntarily separated from the firm, less the deduction that was available up to the end of the previous year; or 6 percent of total payroll costs. However, no tax deduction is allowed if funds are invested outside the firm, which explains why most firms create internal book reserves for lump-sum payments.

Because of the rising cost of lump-sum retirement programs (owing to rising wages, the aging of the population, and the limited deductibility of book reserves), many firms have opted to replace their lump-sum severance packages with pension schemes. More than 80 percent of firms with 1,000 or more employees have transformed their traditional retirement plans, partially or entirely, into funded pensions. (However, because many retirees opt to take their pension benefits in a lump-sum distribution, the effective magnitude of the shift may be overstated.)

Pension (Annuity) Schemes

Japanese pension (as opposed to lump-sum retirement) plans are either tax-qualified pension plans or employee pension funds. Tax-qualified plans are offered by smaller firms and are not coordinated with the social security system. The employee funds are coordinated with the social security system and can be offered only by larger firms.[49] By offering an employee pension fund, a firm is able to opt out of the earnings-related portion of social security. Firms offering tax-qualified pensions may not do so.

Tax-Qualified Pension Plans

Employer contributions to tax-qualified pension plans are treated as a business expense and are therefore fully deductible. Benefits are not taxable for retirees until they are paid. Retirees receive an income

---

[49]Tax-qualified plans are overseen by the Ministry of Finance, while employee pension funds are overseen by the Ministry of Health and Welfare.

tax exemption for lump-sum payments based on years of service. In 1989, the exemption was ¥400,000 a year of service for the first 20 years and ¥700,000 for each year of service beyond that. One-half of the benefits beyond this amount are tax free, while the other half are taxable as regular income. Retirement income from annuities is also subject to preferential (though more complicated) tax treatment. Finally, the assets in a pension plan's reserve fund are taxed at a rate of 1.173 percent a year.

By law, all employees of a firm, except company directors, must be eligible to participate in the retirement fund. Benefits must be based on years of service, using either a flat benefit or an earnings-related formula. Most plans offer fixed-term annuities of 5, 10, or 15 years, rather than life annuities, with no joint or survivor options. The interest rate used to convert fixed-term annuities to lump-sum values is specified by the Ministry of Finance. Because this rate, which has been set at 5.5 percent for some time, exceeds the rate of interest on government debt, it penalizes retirees electing the lump-sum option. This penalty notwithstanding, 90 percent of retirees opt for the lump-sum payment. Workers who leave the firm before normal retirement age typically must take a lump-sum benefit, because there is no vesting of annuities.

Employer contributions must be either a specific yen amount or a specific percentage of payroll; contributions depend on liabilities measured using service to date and a projection of future earnings based on the tenure-earnings relationship in place in that company at that time. Future inflation and productivity growth are ignored in calculating liabilities. Funding is limited to 100 percent of liabilities, and employee contributions are almost never required. Tax-qualified pension plans must be actuarially evaluated at least every five years, and any excess reserves must be returned to the firm at that time. As a result, pension plans are almost always underfunded because firms are not allowed to make excess contributions to take into account wage growth attributable to productivity enhancements or inflation.

Investment policies are dictated by law. At least 50 percent of funds must be in government bonds or bonds carrying a government guarantee. At most, 30 percent can be in stocks, 30 percent in foreign investments, and 20 percent in real estate. Finally, no more than 10 percent of the pension fund can be invested in the sponsoring company.

Employee Pension Funds

Employee pension funds can cover workers in a single company or in two or more companies. Because of minimum size regulations established by the government, these funds are much larger than tax-qualified pension funds. Both employer and employee contributions are tax exempt. Although the assets of funds are in theory taxable, the exemption level is set high enough that the assets of most funds are exempt.

Benefits are composed of two parts. The first, the "substitution" component, is linked to the earnings-related component of the social security system, the employees' pension insurance payment. Its name reflects the fact that, in exchange for lower social security contributions, the employee pension funds take responsibility for providing the earnings-related component of social security. Contributions to fund these payments are shared equally by the firm and its employees.

The second benefit component is a supplemental payment, to be provided by the employee pension fund, that should equal at least 30 percent of the substitution benefit that employees accrue while working for the firm. Employer contributions to the supplementary payment must be at least as large as those required of employees. As with tax-qualified pension plans, an interest rate of 5.5 percent is used to calculate the lump-sum value of a retirement annuity. The government takes responsibility for cost of living increases to the substitution benefit. No cost of living increases are typically granted for the supplemental benefit.

Workers are fully vested for the substitution benefit after one month of employment. Vesting for the supplementary benefit typically occurs after 20 years of employment, although reduced lump-sum payments are available to those who separate from firms early. The Pension Fund Association (PFA), of which all employee pension funds are required to be members, takes responsibility for paying the substitution benefit to workers who leave their employers after fewer than ten years, with the assets sufficient to make these payments transferred from the firm's pension fund to the PFA's accounts. Thus, the PFA provides for portability of the contracted-out benefit. In addition, workers have the option of transferring their lump-sum supplemental severance payment to the PFA for a future life annuity that is actuarially equivalent to the lump sum.

Funding and administration are supervised by the Ministry of Health and Welfare. Funds are held and invested by either trust banks or insurance companies, although consideration has been given to allowing the use of investment advisors and in-house management. Investment policies are identical to those prescribed for tax-qualified pension plans. As with tax-qualified plans, liabilities are determined by projecting earnings out to retirement using the company's current tenure-earnings profile. Funding is limited to 100 percent of liabilities, with actuarial reviews occurring at least once every five years. However, excess reserves are not returned to the sponsoring firm. Instead, firms must either reduce future contributions or improve plan benefits, with either change requiring the approval of the Ministry of Health and Welfare.

Employee pension funds are organized as public corporations and are established by employers and employees. A majority of employees and unions must approve their establishment. They are managed by large governing bodies (14–68 members), with employers and employees each choosing the same number of members.

United Kingdom

A wide variety of occupational pension schemes are in place in the United Kingdom, to which about one-half of the workforce contributes, a level of coverage that has remained steady since the mid-1960s. By one estimate, private pension funds account for about one-third of all personal wealth in the United Kingdom and hold about 40 percent of all U.K. equities (Dilnot and Johnson, 1993).

Occupational Defined-Benefits Plans

The occupational schemes are required by law to offer a specific guaranteed minimum pension. Most offer more generous pensions, ranging from one-half to two-thirds of final-year earnings. Part of this benefit, up to one and a half times final-year earnings, may be taken as a tax-free lump sum.[50] Except for the onetime lump-sum payment, annual pension benefits cannot exceed two-thirds of final-year salary without endangering the preferred tax treatment for pension contributions. In 1989, the government imposed a limit of £60,000 on pensionable earnings for new plans or new entrants to existing plans. This ceiling is indexed to the retail price index and thus increases annually. Occupational schemes are required to index the guaranteed minimum pension for price increases up to 3 percent a year, with the state assuming responsibility for the costs of any inflation exceeding this rate.

There are few restrictions on the investment practices of pension funds, other than an implicit requirement (through the trustees' duty of prudence) to diversify assets. Not more than 5 percent of a pension fund's assets can be invested in the stock of its sponsoring company. Pension funds must have a sufficient level of funding to cover a guaranteed minimum pension, payment of which is guaranteed by the government in the event that the private scheme fails. However, there is no requirement that plans be funded above this level. In addition, assets are valued not at their current market prices, but rather on the basis of the discounted value of expected future cash flows.

Recently, provisions have been put in place to limit overfunding to 5 percent of projected obligations, require indexation of benefits for early retirees, outlaw compulsory membership, limit tax-free contributions and benefits, and increase portability. These changes are expected to lead to a decline in company-based pension plans because they reduce the attractiveness of the plans to both employees and employers. Nonetheless, no clear trend away from company plans is as yet observable.

Opting Out of the State System and Defined-Contributions Plans

Since 1988, workers and employers have also been allowed to choose individual personal defined-contributions plans, offered through insurance companies, banks, and other financial institutions. Under these schemes, the worker and the employer continue to make full contributions to the State Earnings-Related Pension Plan (the earnings-related component of the public scheme), which are then subsequently transferred to the chosen plan. This opting-out feature reduces contributions to the public system and, in this respect, is similar to the Chilean system, with the important difference that in the United Kingdom participation in defined-contributions plans is not compulsory.

Workers and employers can also make additional, tax-free contributions (within limits) to the scheme, whose value at retirement will depend not only on the value of contributions, but also on the performance of the investments made by the fund. Benefits under these schemes must be indexed for up to 3 percent annual inflation—again, with the state paying the costs resulting from higher inflation. It was expected that these defined-contributions plans would be more popular with employers and thus encourage the spread of private pension schemes. By 1990, about 4 million individuals had opted for personal pension plans (2.7 million of them men), and the take-up rate among men aged 22–26 approached 50 percent.

United States

The private pension system in the United States is massive, with more than 800,000 plans in operation in 1985. According to a 1995 survey, 91 percent of

---

[50]In general, firms limit the amount of final-year earnings that may be taken as a lump sum to three-eightieths for each year of service, so that an individual would need 40 years of tenure to qualify for the maximum lump-sum withdrawal of one and a half times final-year earnings.

firms with more than 200 employees offer some sort of retirement plan. In 1987, nearly 42 million workers—representing 46 percent of private wage and salary earners—were covered by a private pension plan. However, the participation rate for full-time employees has declined over time and, between 1985 and 1988, fell from 91 percent to 86 percent.

At the same time, employer-provided plans (which constitute about four-fifths of all private pension plans) have been shifting from defined-benefits to defined-contributions coverage. In 1975, 87 percent of active participants in private pension plans received their primary coverage through a defined-benefits plan, but by 1985, the percentage had dropped to 71 percent. In 1995, more than half of all firms offered their employees both types of plans. Generally, the larger a firm and the more unionized its employees, the more likely it is to offer a pension program.

To some extent, these changes in the level and type of pension coverage reflect shifts in employment patterns, with the gaining sectors not being as heavily "pensionized" as the losers. However, they also reflect changes in the tax treatment of defined-contributions plans, and possibly also some loss of confidence in the financial integrity of defined-benefits plans.

Few private pension plans index their benefits for inflation. During the 1970s, many beneficiaries of private pensions received ad hoc inflation adjustments, although typically these were not sufficient to maintain the real value of benefits. During the 1980s, only about one-fourth of all participants in medium-size and large firms were in plans that granted post-retirement benefit increases to retirees. This aspect of the private pension system means that it does not really provide a full annuity to retired persons.

Vesting periods vary from program to program. After the passage of the ERISA in 1974, workers were generally vested after ten years of service. The Tax Reform Act of 1986 shortened the allowable vesting period for most workers to a maximum of five years. Typically, defined-contributions plans will have shorter vesting periods than defined-benefits plans. The ERISA also established IRAs, which allowed workers not covered by private pension plans to make tax-deferred contributions of up to $1,500 a year (later raised to $2,000) to a retirement account. In 1981, IRA eligibility was extended to almost all workers, although the Tax Reform Act of 1986 eliminated the ability of higher-income taxpayers to invest pretax dollars— that is, to make tax-deductible investments—in IRAs. In 1985, about 16 percent of all taxpayers contributed to an IRA, but by 1987, after the tax law change, the percentage of participants fell to about 7 percent.

In general, pension contributions are tax deductible when made, and benefits are taxed only when they are received. However, there are upper limits on the size of contributions individuals can deduct from their taxable income, and there is a maximum benefit that defined-benefits plans can pay. In 1982, this limit was $90,000 a year (with cost of living adjustments to this ceiling beginning not in that year but in 1986), and contributions to defined-contributions plans were capped at $30,000 a year, with no inflation adjustment until the maximum defined-benefits pension reached $120,000 a year. The Tax Reform Act of 1986 linked the retirement age for defined-benefits plans to the retirement age for social security pensions, with actuarial reductions in benefits being mandated for early retirement. The 1986 law also capped the annual salary that could be used for calculating either benefits or contributions at $200,000 (to be adjusted for inflation annually) and limited the amount that employees could invest in tax-deferred 401(k) accounts. In 1993, the annual salary cap for pension calculations was rolled back to $150,000 a year. Employee income that is contributed to a retirement program on an after-tax basis is tax exempt when withdrawn, although any income earned on the contribution is taxable when withdrawn. Under the Tax Reform Act of 1986, employees pay a 10 percent excise tax on early distributions. The employer may also pay a penalty tax (in addition to corporate income tax) on any assets that revert to it following the voluntary termination of its retirement program and the distribution of benefits to its employees (e.g., as would be the case if the firm deliberately overfunded its retirement plan to reduce its current tax liability). Perhaps in part as a result of increasing legal restrictions on pension funding, firm contributions to pension plans in the United States fell sharply in the 1980s.

Private pension plans are subject to considerable federal regulation. Federal law requires that firms that offer pension programs do so in a way that does not discriminate among classes of employees. The Tax Reform Act of 1986 establishes a simple test: at least 70 percent of a firm's rank-and-file employees should be eligible to participate in the pension plan, and at least 70 percent of those eligible to participate should do so. Average benefit tests, and a requirement that at least 40 percent of all employees should benefit from the program, also exist. Employees covered by plans must be eligible to participate after one year of employment. In June 1995, the U.S. administration announced plans to weaken some of the criteria used to determine if a plan is discriminatory. Specifically, under the administration's proposal (which must be approved by the Congress), companies with fewer than 100 employees would be exempted from nondiscrimination requirements.

Financial aspects of private pension plans are also subject to federal regulation. The ERISA prohibited unfunded defined-benefits plans and set minimum funding standards that require defined-benefits plans to amortize past service liabilities over 40 years. Experience gains and losses had to be amortized over 15 years, and benefit increases over 30 years. In 1987, the amortization period for existing liabilities was shortened to 18 years, and the payment of funding contributions was changed from an annual to a quarterly basis. Since 1988, experience gains and losses for single-employer plans must be amortized over a five-year period. Defined-benefits plans are insured by the Pension Benefit Guarantee Board, with the plans paying insurance premiums. Benefits from defined-contributions plans are entirely at risk.

Pension Plans in Selected Countries Introducing a Chilean-Style System

Argentina

Public Scheme

Prior to the 1994 Reform

Pension benefits have historically been generous in Argentina: prior to the reforms that were introduced in 1994, individuals who had worked for at least 30 years and contributed to the system for at least 20 years qualified for a pension at the statutory retirement age of 60 for males and 55 for females (65 and 60 if self-employed). The retirement age as well as contribution and employment requirements were lowered or relaxed by up to ten years for hazardous or unhealthy occupations. Pensioners could continue to work after retirement with full benefits, except that pensions were not recalculated to include post-retirement income. Special programs (e.g., for the legislative branch and the judiciary) and provincial pension systems allowed retirement on extremely generous terms and are now in financial distress as a result. Disability pensions were readily granted. Workers who had contributed for at least five years and who had a work history of ten years were eligible for an old-age pension.

Before 1994, pensions were set at 70–82 percent of the base wage, depending on the age of retirement. The pensionable base was calculated as the average of the worker's three highest annual wages during the ten years prior to retirement. Pensions were in principle fully indexed. In practice, indexation was ad hoc, and over time the real value of pensions suffered a substantial decline. Thus, the real value of pensions declined by 25 percent between 1981 and 1988 and by another 30 percent from 1988 to 1991. Pensions could not exceed 15 times the minimum pension set by the government. The minimum pension was not automatically indexed to inflation, despite the country's bouts with hyperinflation, but was adjusted on an ad hoc basis. The deterioration in the financial position of the system is essentially explained by the erosion in the contribution base—to which high payroll tax rates contributed—generous pension benefits, and demography. The economic crisis of the 1980s aggravated the financial position of the public scheme, and, by 1990, the pension fund had accumulated a substantial amount of arrears to pensioners.[51]

Reform of 1994

The social security reform adopted in October 1993 (which became operational in July 1994 and was modified in January 1995) kept the old system in place, albeit with reduced benefits, and gave participants a onetime option of participating in the new mixed public-private pension system (described below). The Argentine public scheme now consists of three parts:

- the "universal benefit": a basic pension with a flat component and a component that varies in proportion to the years of contributions in excess of 30;
- a "compensatory benefit": an earnings-related pension amounting to 1.5 percent of the individual's average indexed monthly salary of the last ten years of contributions times the number of years of contributions made before July 1994, up to a maximum of 35 years or 52.5 percent of average indexed salary; and
- an optional "staying benefit": those who choose to stay in the public scheme receive 0.85 percent of their final ten-year average monthly salary for every year of contributions made after July 1994.

Those individuals who switch to the new capitalization regime forgo the staying benefit. As explained below, these workers make payments into a personal account held at a specialized financial insti-

---

[51]In 1991, the government took some important steps to improve the system's financial position: (1) the minimum contribution period required for a pension was raised to 20 years form 15 years and the contribution rate was increased to 26 percent from 21 percent; (2) the consolidation of pension arrears was begun by issuing "consolidation bonds" with a ten-year maturity. In 1991, improved collection efforts helped to stem the accumulation of pension arrears. In April 1993, the Federal Tax Administration was made responsible for social security collections, which further improved collections.

tution. Upon retirement, they gain access to the amounts accumulated in those accounts.

Pensions are no longer indexed but are revised every year during the budget discussions. Individuals who have reached retirement age but are not covered by the system are entitled to a public assistance pension (subject to a means test) that is financed from general revenue. The retirement ages in both schemes will increase gradually to 65 for men and 60 for women.[52]

Contribution rates are now set at 11 percent for employees and 16 percent for employers;[53] the self-employed pay 27 percent. There is no ceiling on the earnings on which contributions are calculated. In agricultural activities, the insured's contribution is replaced by a sales tax on agricultural produce. The government also contributes to social security through general revenues and certain earmarked taxes.

Pension income does not enjoy especially generous tax treatment in Argentina, and pension income in excess of the minimum pension is subject to income tax. In Argentina, less than 2 percent of social security expenditures are spent on administration of the old-age, survivors', and disability pensions. This is the lowest level of all Latin American countries. Other countries with relatively broad systems, like Chile (4.8 percent) and Costa Rica (4.6 percent), have incurred much higher administrative costs.[54]

Private Sector Participation Under the Recent Reform

The major innovation introduced by the 1994 reform was a second tier, a feature inspired by the Chilean reform. The above-described reformed public pension system remained in place, but the worker's 11 percent mandatory social security contribution finances the second tier should he choose to participate.[55] The first tier is a PAYG scheme, while the second is a fully funded defined-contributions plan, privately administered and publicly regulated by the superintendency for pension funds. Individuals may choose to remain entirely within the public system (on the terms already described) or to

opt for what amounts to a mixed system by contributing their share of the payroll tax to an individual capitalization account managed by a private pension fund. The employer's contribution continues to go to the public scheme.

The reform does not entail the gradual elimination of the public scheme, inasmuch as the private scheme supplements but does not replace the public scheme. In contrast to the Chilean system, contributions are uniform for the whole system. The compensatory benefit serves the same function as Chile's recognition bond, but rather than being deposited by the state as a lump sum in an individual deposit account, it is paid by the public scheme to the contributor once retired.

Between September 1994 and June 1995, the number of people covered under the social security scheme rose from 5.7 million to 7 million (about half the labor force), of which 55 percent were enrolled in the mixed system. Compliance in both systems has been weak: only 54 percent of those insured under the mixed scheme were active contributors, in contrast to 71 percent under the public scheme.

In addition to the complementary nature of the Argentine scheme, it differs from the Chilean system in other ways:

- Contributions are collected by the social security system, instead of one of the pension companies.
- Private pension funds are granted greater latitude in their investment decisions than in Chile.
- The superintendency for pension funds is financed by the pension funds (not by the state, as in Chile).
- The state is responsible for paying the life annuity to the pensioner if an insurance company goes bankrupt (not available in Chile).

Colombia

Public Scheme

Colombia's pension system is one of the most fragmented in Latin America; it includes a large number of pension plans (about 1,000) with a wide variety of benefits and low contribution levels. At one time, public sector agencies, including state-owned enterprises, were allowed to offer their own pension plans, which tended to be much more generous than the plan of the social security institute (ISS). In 1993, the total number of contributors in all plans (4.2 million) reached 30 percent of Colombia's labor force, or 32 percent of total employment. About 70 percent of those covered were under the ISS, 5 percent were under the civil servants' social security institute (CAJANAL), and the rest were covered by specialized public sector employee plans. The sys-

---

[52]The retirement ages rose to 63 and 58 in 1996 and will rise to 64 and 59 in 1998 and 65 and 60 in 2001.

[53]In 1994, employer contributions were reduced by between 30 percent and 80 percent of the statutory rate of 16 percent, depending on the location of employment.

[54]The figure for Chile is for the old state-run and the new privately administered systems together.

[55]About 70 percent of the employee's contribution goes to his individual account, and the rest covers administrative fees and disability insurance premiums.

tem's coverage is comparatively low for a country of Colombia's per capita income level.[56]

Benefits for civil service workers are very generous, and entitlement conditions quite liberal. The retirement age is 10 years lower than in the ISS, which is in turn quite low: 60 for males and 55 for females. In some public plans, retirement is possible with only 10–20 years of service, regardless of age. Eligibility for an old-age pension under the ISS system requires at least 1,000 weeks of contributions.

The basic pension under the ISS system is set at 65 percent of base earnings plus an increment of 2 percent for each 50 weeks over 1,000 weeks of contributions up to 1,200 weeks.[57] The increment is increased to 3 percent for each 50 weeks over 1,200 and up to 1,400 weeks. Pensions cannot exceed the lesser of 85 percent of the basic monthly wage or 20 times the minimum monthly wage. The minimum pension is set equal to the minimum wage. Pensions in Colombia are indexed to wages and adjusted annually.

Old-age pensions were financed by a payroll tax that averaged about 11.5 percent of the monthly salary in 1994 (12.5 percent in 1995 and 13.5 percent in 1996); the employer paid 75 percent of these contributions and the employee paid 25 percent. Before 1994, contribution rates averaged only about 6.5 percent. Employees who earn the equivalent of at least four monthly minimum wages a month must contribute an additional 1 percent of their salaries. A ceiling of 20 minimum salaries applies to the contribution base. Statutory contribution rates to CAJANAL and to other public sector employee pension plans are substantially lower (often zero). Moreover, actual contributions paid by government employees to CAJANAL and public sector employee plans have been insignificant, contributing to the system's financial imbalance.

The ISS did not conduct any formal actuarial reviews in the 1980s. Recent actuarial valuations have revealed substantial actuarial deficits in both the ISS and CAJANAL. During the 1980s, the ISS pension reserves were invested in government bonds at a fixed nominal interest rate, which resulted in negative real rates of return. Moreover, the ISS was forced to finance the health component of the social security system. By 1991, reserves in both institutions were almost depleted. In 1992, accrued outstanding obligations of the ISS (the present value of anticipated payments net of contributions) were equivalent to 29 percent of GDP, while the stock of reserves amounted to only 1.6 percent of GDP. The contribution rate required to put the system back on even a partially funded basis was 18 percent for 1992–95, rising to 21 percent for 1996–2000. Pension administration is grossly inefficient.[58]

Contributions to pension plans paid by employers are tax deductible for the employer and not taxable for the employee, while contributions paid by employees are deductible from taxable income.

Recent Reforms and Private Pension Funds

The April 1994 pension reform (passed in December 1993) aimed to forestall the increase in the actuarial deficit of the ISS, CAJANAL, and the remaining funds and to increase their coverage. The reform of the pension system closely follows the Chilean model.[59] Workers may choose to shift from the public to an individual capitalization account system, which, as in Chile, is publicly regulated and privately administered by pension fund administrators. Alternatively, they may remain in the ISS, which will become a partially funded, defined-benefits plan.[60] Finally, government workers covered by solvent public sector funds may remain with them.

Contribution rates for the private system are the same as in the ISS. Since 1996, the contribution rate has been 13.5 percent of the wage base, 10 percent of which goes to the individual's retirement account and 3.5 percent to administrative expenses and insurance premiums (for privately administered funds). An additional 1 percent of pensionable wages is still paid by all employees with wages greater than four times the minimum wage. This additional contribution is deposited in the Pension Solidarity Fund to help cover pension contributions for those who are unable to pay even the contribution required of a minimum wage earner. A recognition bond will be issued for those who switch to the new system to account for their years of contributions to the old system; this bond will be indexed to the consumer price index (CPI) and will earn interest at a rate of 3–4 percent a year. The present value of these bonds is estimated at about 18 percent of GDP. There is a minimum pension guarantee by the government for participants in the new system.

---

[56]World Bank (1984) presents cross-country regressions linking pension coverage to per capita income. The results predict pension coverage in Colombia equal to 43 percent of the labor force, about one-third higher than actual.

[57]Base earnings are defined as the inflation-adjusted average income over the preceding ten years.

[58]World Bank (1993).

[59]See Schmidt-Hebbel (1995) for a detailed analysis of the reform.

[60]The partial funding of the defined-benefits plan will be achieved through a combination of higher contribution rates, lower benefits, and later retirement ages for younger workers.

The reform also includes increases in the retirement age to 62 for men and 57 for women by 2014 as well as measures to tighten eligibility requirements and benefits of the ISS system. Insolvent public employee plans—which constitute a large majority of funds for public employees—are being closed, and their contributors are being offered a choice of affiliating with the ISS or the private system. The law makes no other changes to CAJANAL or other public sector employee pension plans. New labor market entrants have mandatory coverage under their choice of the ISS or the private system, implying that the old systems for public sector employees will be phased out over the next 40 years. As of about end-1994, about 20 percent of the state plans' participants had opted to move to the new system, in which eight pension fund administrators were functioning.

Contributions made by an employer to individual capitalization accounts not exceeding 13.5 percent of the salary paid to the employee are excluded from the taxable income of the beneficiary. The excess over 10 percent is, however, included in employment income subject to the income withholding tax. Pensions less than 20 times the minimum wage are exempt. Consequently, pension saving receives highly favorable tax treatment.

Mexico

Mexico is about to enter the crucial stage of the reform of its social security system. The largest element of the present pension system, a publicly managed PAYG-financed plan for private sector workers, has been replaced, as of July 1, 1997, with a privately managed defined-contributions plan. The design of the Mexican reform calls for all participants in the old plan to begin contributing to the new plan as if they were new entrants to the labor market. In this respect, it differs from the Chilean model. However, current participants will have the option of retiring under the provisions of the old plan. This option will not be open to young workers. As explained below, the Mexican reform has some other special features that distinguish it from the reforms introduced in other countries.

Current System

The existing system has three pillars. The first pillar consists of a set of publicly managed, mandatory PAYG plans that provide benefits for old age, disability, unemployment in old age (before retirement age is reached), and death (called IVCM plans—*invalidez, vejez, cesantía en edad avanzada, y muerte*). The most important plans in this category are the plan for private sector workers (managed by the Mexican Social Security Institute, IMSS) and the plan for gov-

ernment employees (administered by the Institute for Social Security and Services for State Workers, ISSSTE). Other plans cover specialized groups of public sector employees, such as the oil company workers and the military. The IMSS and ISSSTE are each supplemented by a mandatory housing-saving fund (INFONAVIT and FOVISSSTE, respectively), which have offered a minimum return guarantee since 1992.[61]

The second pillar, which is also mandatory, consists of individual retirement accounts (SARs) for workers in both the public and the private sectors that are financed by an employee payroll tax, managed by commercial banks, and supported by a minimum-return government guarantee. About 8,000 occupational pension plans constitute the third pillar of the system.[62]

The public PAYG plans are the largest element of the current arrangement. These plans cover about 45 percent of the workforce: the IMSS has 10 million contributors; the ISSSTE, 1.5 million; the PEMEX plan, 0.5 million; and the plan for the military, 0.3 million. The institutions managing these IVCM plans also administer health care, maternity benefits, work-accident insurance, and other benefits for contributors and their families.

The IVCM plan for private sector workers is financed with contributions adding up to 8.5 percent of the gross wage (5.95 percent is paid by the employer, 2.125 by the employee, and 0.425 by the government), with a ceiling of ten minimum wages on the portion of the wage used for computing the contribution. The public sector workers' IVCM is financed by a contribution of 7 percent of their gross wage, subject to the same ceiling. Additional contributions of 5 percent and 6 percent of the wage are made to the corresponding housing funds, INFONAVIT and FOVISSSTE.[63] The SAR is financed with a 2 percent payroll tax paid by employers.

---

[61]The housing funds can be said to play a complementary role in the sense that, upon retirement, workers are eligible to receive the unused portion of their accumulated contributions to the funds. They also receive the amounts accumulated in their individual accounts under the SARs.

[62]The law does not require the existence of an occupational pension plan as part of the normal labor relationship. The plans may or may not be voluntary for the individual worker depending on the characteristics of the plan itself. The law allows employers to buy additional benefits for their workers by transferring additional contributions to the IMSS; the additional contributions for the desired additional benefits are determined by the IMSS using actuarial techniques, and are then incorporated into collective contracts on the one hand and into a contract between the employer and the IMSS on the other. Any change in the collective contract that affects the original terms of the additional insurance would prompt a review of the contract between the employer and the IMSS.

[63]Health and other benefits provided by the IMSS and ISSSTE are funded with additional contributions of 12.5 percent and 9.5 percent of the gross wage, respectively.

Workers become eligible to retire with a full pension under the IVCM plans upon reaching age 65 and after having made contributions for at least 500 weeks.[64] Monthly benefits are computed with a formula that takes into account the length of the contribution period and earnings during an individual's final five years of work,[65] but a minimum pension equal to 95 percent of one minimum wage is guaranteed (about 80 percent of the pensions paid by the IMSS are given at the minimum level). IVCM pensions are adjusted in proportion to the minimum wage and include Christmas bonuses.

Reform of 1997

The reform of July 1997 will initially affect only the IMSS-administered PAYG plan for private sector workers; the rest of the pension system will remain unchanged. That PAYG plan will be replaced by a privately managed defined-contributions plan. The reform will split the IVCM plan in two parts: the disability and life insurance parts will remain with the IMSS, while the old-age, old-age unemployment, and retirement parts (known now as RCV—*retiro, cesantía, y vejez*) will be managed by private sector firms called AFOREs—Administradoras de Fondos de Ahorro para el Retiro. The AFOREs will administer individual capitalization accounts built up with participants' contributions. (Accumulated balances in INFONAVIT and the SARs are expected to be transferred to the individual's account held with an AFORE; however, INFONAVIT funds will be kept in a subaccount and will continue to be available to finance the purchase of a dwelling.)

Under the reform, current pensioners will continue to receive their pension from the IMSS on current terms. New workers—defined as those who have never contributed to the IMSS—will contribute to the new plan from the start and will retire under it. Workers who have contributed to the IMSS—called transition workers—will switch to the new plan and start contributing to it as soon as it is operational. Their individual accounts will be credited with their accumulated contributions to the SARs and the INFONAVIT,

but there will be no explicit recognition of their past contributions to the IMSS scheme. Instead, transition workers will retain the option of retiring under the benefits of the old IMSS scheme, including their accumulated contributions to INFONAVIT and their SAR balances accumulated over 1993–96 (in this case, when they retire, they will turn the balance in their capitalization accounts over to the IMSS).

Contributions under the new RCV systems will be 6.5 percent of the worker's wage, plus a government contribution of Mex\$1.00 a day (the "social quota"). Additionally, the INFONAVIT subaccount continues to receive 5 percent of the wage, and the IMSS will still get 4 percent of the wage to finance disability and life insurance (the part of the old IVCM that it retains under the reform). Under the new arrangement, total contributions will exceed the level of contributions under the old arrangement (IVCM plus SAR and INFONAVIT) by the amount of the social quota. The cap on the salary used for calculating contributions will be increased to 25 times the minimum wage under the reform.

When individuals retire, benefits will consist of the accumulated AFORE balances, including the INFONAVIT subaccount (transition workers also get back their 1993–96 SAR balances). AFORE balances can be withdrawn gradually or used to purchase an annuity from an insurance company. The new system will be supported by a government guarantee of a minimum pension equal to one minimum wage as of January 1, 1997, indexed to the CPI. Under the new system, workers will become eligible to retire at age 65 (age 60 if unemployed), but to be eligible to benefit from the minimum pension guarantee, they must contribute for at least 1,250 weeks.

It is difficult to determine whether saving rates will increase as a result of the reform, largely because the reform's impact on the budget constraints of system participants is hard to determine. The reform will increase the ceiling for calculating contributions to 25 times from 10 times the minimum wage, which should increase involuntary saving. However, total payroll taxes earmarked for the financing of pension schemes would drop by almost 1 percentage point, which would have the opposite effect.[66] The freedom

---

[64]A reduced pension is available for system participants who have contributed during the requisite period and become involuntarily unemployed between the ages of 60 and 64. If they choose to claim this benefit, they will not be able to claim a full pension later on.

[65]The formula is such that benefits are the sum of a "basic amount," which is approximately equal to 80 percent of one minimum wage, and an "increment for years." The increment is computed by multiplying three factors: (1) a worker's average wage over the final five years of contributions, (2) the number of years of contributions in excess of the minimum contribution period of ten years, and (3) a factor (between 0.56 and 2.4 percent) that varies positively with average income. For any given contribution period (longer than ten years), the increment for years grows faster than average income, and for any given average income, it grows in proportion to the excess contribution period.

[66]Worker and employer contributions to the IVCM and the SARs under the current law add up to 10.075 percent of the wage, while their combined contributions to the disability and life scheme and to the old-age and old-age unemployment scheme (including the retirement account) under the new law add up to 9.125 percent of the wage (contributions to the housing-saving fund are unchanged). Because of the practice of consolidating the contributions to each component of the IVCM scheme, it is not possible to make an exact comparison of the rates for the old-age pension component under the old and new systems. Further obscuring this comparison, take-home pay is also affected by the change in the contributions to the health insurance and workers' compensation schemes, where the nature of the formulas, and not just the rates, will change more radically.

of choice given transitional workers to retire under the old or the new system has an important bearing on the reform's impact on benefits. Because the terms of the old system do not change, the freedom to choose may make workers feel better off after the reform (i.e., they may experience a positive wealth effect), which could actually reduce their saving. Transitional workers may also believe that the reform will render their future pensions more secure.

To the extent that the new system is more attractive to the self-employed—who do not now contribute to the IMSS in significant numbers—and to the extent that their contributions are not simply offset by a decline in other forms of saving, their participation in the scheme should raise saving. As discussed in this paper, however, the fiscal consolidation undertaken with the reform is key to its impact on total saving. In particular, the reform's separation of the old-age pension scheme from the social security system could be significant if the new financial structure improves the balance of the latter (the health scheme has a deficit that is partially covered by resources from the IVCM).

Peru

Public Scheme

Before July 1995, Peru's public pension system comprised the general plan (the Peruvian Institute of Social Security (IPSS)), the civil servant pension plan (*cédula viva*), and several specialized public sector plans. In 1992, more than 80 percent of those covered were under the IPSS. Little is known about the benefits and financial position of the specialized public sector plans. The IPSS was providing pensions to workers who had reached the statutory retirement age (60 for men and 55 for women), provided they had contributed for a minimum of 20 years. The coverage of the Peruvian pension system is very narrow (the effective coverage of the labor force is about 30 percent).

In the past, the IPSS suffered dramatic decapitalization in real terms because of negative real investment yields, evasion, and payment delays. It also accumulated substantial arrears to pensioners. In addition, the IPSS has been remarkably costly to administer.

In July 1995, the IPSS was restructured: the responsibility for public pensions was assigned to the Oficina de Normalización Provisional (ONP); health care activities remained under the IPSS. At the same time, the retirement ages were increased to 65 for both men and women.

The basic pension is currently set at 50 percent of the reference salary, which is defined as the average salary a worker earns during the final three years of work. It is increased by 4 percent for each year of contributions over the minimum of 20 years. The maximum monthly benefit is equal to 100 percent of the reference salary, but not more than S/. 600 (about US$300). Pensions are usually adjusted at the time of central government wage increases.

In July 1995, the government increased the ONP's contribution rate from 9 percent to 11 percent. The employer makes no contribution (previously, 6 percent); workers contribute 11 percent (previously 3 percent). Workers' contributions are based on their total monthly remuneration including in-kind benefits—with certain exemptions, notably, participation in profits and extraordinary bonuses. Employees' contributions are tax deductible, as were employers' contributions prior to July 1995.

Benefits under the *cédula viva* are very generous, at least compared with salary levels; most pensioners are entitled to a pension equal to the highest earned pensionable salary. However, the system's administration is inefficient and prone to abuse, as evidenced by the many cases of fraud detected through audits. Under the *cédula viva*, active workers contribute 8–15 percent of their pensionable salary. Only a small fraction of pension benefits are covered by these contributions, so that benefits are financed almost entirely from general revenues, implying a very high implicit rate of return on contributions.

Recent Reforms and Private Pension Funds

Since June 21, 1993, Peruvian workers have been allowed to join a Chilean-style individual capitalization account.[67] The Peruvian private pension plan is a privately managed but publicly regulated defined-contributions plan. Upon reaching retirement age, workers may choose from a range of pension options. The value of the annuity or lump-sum combination they choose depends on the value of the contributions they made during their working life and the investment experience of the pension company (Administradoras de Fondos de Pensiones (AFP)) managing the funds. Affiliation with the private plan is voluntary for new entrants to the labor force, implying that the existing schemes are not automatically phased out, as they would be under the Chilean model. By the end of October 1995, about 40 percent of IPSS participants had opted to move to the new private plan.

In July 1995, the government passed legislation designed to increase the popularity of the private pension plan. First, contribution rates and retirement

---

[67]Civil service workers belonging to the *cédula viva* system cannot switch to the private scheme.

ages in the IPSS and the private plan were set approximately equal to one another (the contribution rate for the latter was lowered from 15 percent to 11.6 percent). Second, to increase competition, workers were now allowed to move freely and without penalty between AFPs. Third, the new legislation contemplates the introduction of a minimum pension for those in the private plan whose pension would fall below a certain threshold.

Under the private plan, employees contribute 8 percent of their total pay to their individual capitalization account (plus additional commissions to cover invalidity, survivors' pensions, and administrative costs that together amount to about 3.6 percent. Employers make no contribution, although they are obliged to increase the pay of existing employees who opt to join the private plan, which they can do without loss because contributions to the ONP are no longer required.

To encourage long-time IPSS contributors to move to the private pension plan, a recognition bond based on the work history of each individual is issued to them for credit to their account at retirement. Because of the lack of reliable records, a simple formula was defined to calculate the value of the bonds.[68] The present value of these bonds is calculated at about US$4 billion.

Workers may contribute up to 20 percent of their employment income (including the mandatory 11.6 percent) to their individual capitalization account. These supplementary contributions are not tax deductible; however, pension income is tax exempt.

Uruguay

Public Scheme

Before the 1995 social security reform, Uruguay's mandatory PAYG social security system was one of the most extensive in Latin America. The system comprised the Social Security Bank (Banco de Previsión Social (BPS)), the special retirement plans for the police and the military, and three employee-run plans for bank employees, notaries, and professionals.[69] Total outlays of the social security system—in-

cluding retirement, disability, and old-age pensions; health care; unemployment insurance; and family allowances—were almost 18 percent of GDP in 1994. Of this, outlays for pensions by the BPS alone were about 10 percent of GDP, and by the other plans about 3.5 percent.

For a mature social security system, Uruguay's dependency ratio of contributors to pensioners is one of the lowest in the world. As of 1995, about 70 percent of the labor force (of 1.4 million) contributed to the system, albeit not necessarily at the legally mandated levels, implying, in light of the number of pensioners noted above, a dependency ratio of 1.4. However, adjusting for the fact that some double-dipping took place and that the average old-age and disability pensions was less than half the average retirement pension, the ratio of contributors to effective pensioners was about 1.9.[70]

According to a 1989 constitutional amendment, all pension outlays are indexed to movements in the national wage index. Pensions are adjusted three times a year with a lag of four months.

Under the old BPS plan, average pensions were relatively low, although the number of pensions per capita was high, at about 20 percent. The statutory replacement rate ranged from 60 percent to 75 percent for men, and from 65 percent to 80 percent for women, depending upon years of contribution and age of retirement. There was a ceiling on monthly pensions equal to 7 minimum salaries (currently US$630) and 15 minimum salaries (US$1,225) for all BPS support payments. In 1995, the average retirement pension was only about US$280 a month; the average old-age pension, US$110; and the average disability pension, US$135. These pensions compared with a standard (not minimum) monthly cost of living estimate of over US$1,000 a month.

Since 1979, the minimum retirement age for the social security system (excluding the plans for the police and military) has been 60 for men and 55 for women. The expected life spans of men and women who reach retirement age are 76 and 81 years, respectively; hence, pensions are paid out, on average, for many years.

The combination of an aged population, early retirement ages, comparatively easy entitlement conditions, and an inefficient administration helps explain why the BPS plan generated deficits on the order of 7 percent of GDP (excluding earmarked value-added tax (VAT) revenues and transfers). Administrative shortcomings existed on both the collection and ex-

---

[68]The value of the bond is a function only of the age of the contributor and a reference value that is the same for all contributors.

[69]The BPS plan, according to the latest data, covers about 594,000 people: 360,000 retirees, 62,000 old-age pensioners, and 172,000 other retirees—mainly disability pensioners. The retirement plans for the police and military cover about 30,000 (14,000 retirees and 16,000 pensioners) and 40,000 (23,500 retirees and 16,500 pensioners), respectively. The three employee-run plans together cover about 20,900 (11,400 retirees and 9,500 pensioners). To put these numbers into perspective, Uruguay's total population in 1994 was 3.2 million. Consequently, about 21½ percent of the population receives a pension from one of the plans.

[70]This ratio is not uniform across retirement plans; the dependency ratios are, for the military, 1.06; for the police, 1.24; for bank workers, 1.65; for the BPS, 1.97; for notaries, 5.57; and for professionals, 5.58.

penditure sides. Tax evasion was estimated at one-third of potential revenues (2.5 percent of GDP), and the requirement that individuals must have 30 years of contribution to the system for pension eligibility was widely evaded.

The pensions offered by the special retirement plans are more lucrative. The average retirement pension for professionals is about US$1,500 a month; for bank workers and notaries, US$700. Average monthly police and military retirement pay is low, US$200 and US$270, respectively; however, retirement can be taken after 20 years of service. Furthermore, the pension of retired commissioned military officers can be increased to that of a higher rank if it is determined that they would have achieved this rank had they remained on active duty. Under this regime, a significant number of military retirees collect more in pensions than they earned while serving.

The BPS and the police and military plans have been funded through a 37.5 percent tax on wages, of which 17 percentage points have been paid by employees and 20.5 percentage points by employers. Of these amounts, 13 and 14.5 percentage points, respectively, go for pensions.[71] The remainder goes for health and unemployment insurance and family allowances. Actual collections amount to 8.5 percent of GDP: 7 percent from the private sector, the remainder from public sector employment. The BPS has also been funded through the earmarking of 7 of the 23 percentage points of the VAT (almost 3 percent of GDP) and transfers out of general revenues. The police and military plans run substantial deficits (in 1994 a combined US$250 million, or 1.6 percent of GDP), which are covered by general revenue transfers from the central administration. The employee-run plans are funded through—in addition to the plan-specific wage deductions—special taxes (e.g., a 3 percent tax on notarized contracts) and endowments set up under previous governments.

Employers' contributions to public pension funds are deductible from the corporate income tax. There is no personal income tax in Uruguay.

Recent Reforms and Private Pension Funds

The government approved a reform of the BPS plan in September 1995.[72] The new regime took effect January 1, 1996. The objectives of the BPS reform are to put BPS finances on a sustainable path, reduce labor costs through benefit reductions, im-

prove tax administration, and, eventually, cut the employer contribution rate.

The new BPS plan has two tiers. The first is a reformed version of the present PAYG plan, which is designed to provide a basic pension; this would be supplemented by the second, a capitalized and funded scheme.

The first tier has a uniform retirement age for men and women of 60. For pensions, the pensionable base is the larger of the retiree's average earnings of the final 20 years or the average of the final 10 years, but the latter can be no more than 5 percent larger than the former. The minimum contribution period has been raised to 35 years. The replacement ratio has been reduced significantly for those who retire before age 65—to 52.5 percent from 65 percent for men, and to 52.5 percent from 70 percent for women. For men retiring at age 65, the replacement rate is relatively unchanged at 65 percent; but for women the rate is reduced to 67.5 percent from 80 percent. Replacement rates rise by 3 percent for each year of retirement delayed beyond age 65 and by ½ of 1 percent for each year of contribution beyond 35 to a maximum of 40. The result is a maximum replacement rate for women of 85 percent, which would correspond to a person retiring at age 70 after having contributed for 40 years.

The minimum age for the old-age pension is a uniform 70 years for men and women (it was 65 for the latter), and this pension is available to those who, not qualifying for the benefits described in the previous paragraph, have nevertheless contributed for at least 15 years (compared with 10 years previously). The replacement rate is 55 percent of the pensionable base with a 1 percentage point hike for every year of contribution in excess of 15, up to a maximum of 14 years. Those who contributed for less than 15 years are eligible for a minimum pension when they reach the age of 70. Replacement rates for disability pensions have been reduced to 65 percent from 70 percent.

In addition to these structural changes, there are numerous administrative improvements, the most important of which is the implementation of a system of individual accounts that should allow for better cross-checking of contributions and payments.

Eligibility for the second tier depends upon age. For those under 40, all 13 percentage points of the employee wage tax on total earnings *must* be placed in the capitalized system. For those 40 or older, contributing to the capitalized system is optional. BPS plan contributors who shift to the capitalized plan are eligible for a reduced pension from the PAYG system of 75 percent of the pension to which they would have been entitled had they remained in the system—making a transfer quite attractive for regular contributors to the BPS.

---

[71]In June 1995, the employer contribution for manufacturing enterprises was reduced by 6 percentage points, to 14.5 percent.

[72]In early 1997, draft laws were submitted to the congress to reform the pension systems of the police and military and the three special regimes.

In the absence of the reform, the BPS's financial imbalances would have continued to widen, with outlays growing from almost 15 percent of GDP in 1995 to about 17 percent of GDP by 2035, and with a corresponding increase in transfers from the treasury (including earmarked VAT revenue) from 7 percent of GDP in 1995 to about 9 percent of GDP in 2035. The reform is projected to reduce the BPS plan's outlays to 10 percent of GDP by 2035, while the capitalized element of the reform could reduce BPS revenue by about ¾ of 1 percent of GDP by 2035—to just over 7 percent of GDP. Under the conservative assumption that the new system will cut evasion by one-third, the burden on the treasury will be reduced to just under 2 percent of GDP by 2035, less than the level of earmarked VAT revenue. Thus, with earmarking continued at current legal levels, some of the saving could be used to reduce the heavy tax burden on labor.

References

Auerbach, Alan J., and Laurence J. Kotlikoff, 1983, "An Examination of Empirical Tests of Social Security and Savings," in *Social Policy Evaluation: An Economic Perspective,* ed. by E. Helpman, A. Razin, and E. Sadka (New York: Academic Press).

———, 1995, *Macroeconomics: An Integrated Approach* (Cincinnati, Ohio: South-Western College Publishing).

Avery, Robert B., Gregory E. Elliehausen, and Thomas A. Gustafson, 1986, "Pensions and Social Security in Household Portfolios: Evidence from the 1983 Survey of Consumer Finances," in *Savings and Capital Formation: The Policy Options,* ed. by F.G. Adams and S.M. Wachter (Lexington, Massachusetts: Lexington Books).

Barr, Nicholas, 1993, *The Economics of the Welfare State* (Stanford, California: Stanford University Press).

Barro, R.J., and G. MacDonald, 1979, "Social Security and Consumer Spending in an International Cross Section," *Journal of Public Economics,* Vol. 11 (June), pp. 275–89.

Barros, David, 1979, "Private Saving and the Provision of Social Security in Britain, 1946–75," in *Social Security Versus Private Saving,* ed. by G. von Furstenberg (Cambridge, Massachusetts: Ballinger).

Bernheim, B. Douglas, and John Karl Scholz, 1993, "Private Saving and Public Policy," in *Tax Policy and the Economy,* Vol. 7, ed. by J.M. Poterba (Cambridge, Massachusetts: MIT Press).

Blanchard, Olivier J., and Stanley Fischer, 1989, *Lectures on Macroeconomics* (Cambridge, Massachusetts: MIT Press).

Blinder, Alan S., Roger H. Gordon, and Donald E. Wise, 1980, "Reconsidering the Work Disincentive Effects of Social Security," *National Tax Journal,* Vol. 33 (December), pp. 431–42.

Blum, Ulrich, and Marc Gaudry, 1987, "The Impact of Social Security Contributions on Savings: An Analysis of German Households by Category Using Flexible Econometric Forms," CRDE cahier 2187 (Montreal, Canada: Université de Montreal, Centre de recherche et développement en économique).

Bovenberg, A. Lans, 1989, "Tax Incentives and International Capital Flows: The Case of the United States and Japan," IMF Working Paper 89/5 (Washington: International Monetary Fund).

Burkhauser, Richard, and John Turner, 1982, "Social Security, Preretirement Labor Supply, and Saving: A Confirmation and a Critique," *Journal of Political Economy,* Vol. 90 (June), pp. 643–46.

Cagan, Philip, 1965, *The Effect of Pension Plans on Aggregate Saving: Evidence from a Sample Survey,* NBER Occasional Paper 95 (Cambridge, Massachusetts: National Bureau of Economic Research).

Canziani, Patrizia, and Dimitri Demekas, 1995, "The Italian Public Pension System: Current Prospects and Reform Options," IMF Working Paper 95/33 (Washington: International Monetary Fund).

Chand, Sheetal K., and Albert Jaeger, 1996, *Aging Populations and Public Pension Schemes,* IMF Occasional Paper 147 (Washington: International Monetary Fund).

Chang, Chen Yoke, 1995, "Malaysia's Experience with Provident and Pension Systems" (unpublished; Paris: Organization for Economic Cooperation and Development).

Denny, Michael, and S.A. Rea, 1979, "Pensions and Saving in Canada," in *Social Security Versus Private Saving,* ed. by G. von Furstenberg (Cambridge, Massachusetts: Ballinger).

Diamond, P.A., 1996, "Proposals to Restructure Social Security," in *Journal of Economic Perspectives,* Vol. 10 (Summer), pp. 67–88.

———, and Jerry A. Hausman, 1984, "Individual Retirement and Savings Behavior," *Journal of Public Economics,* Vol. 23 (February–March), pp. 81–114.

Diamond, P.A., and Salvador Valdés-Prieto, 1994, "Social Security Reforms," in *The Chilean Economy: Policy Lessons and Challenges,* ed. by B.P. Bosworth, R. Dornbusch, and R. Labán (Washington: Brookings Institution).

Dicks-Mireaux, Louis, and Mervyn King, 1984, "Pension Wealth and Household Savings: Tests of Robustness," *Journal of Public Economics,* Vol. 23 (February–March), pp. 115–39.

Dilnot, A.W., and Paul A. Johnson, 1993, *The Taxation of Private Pensions* (London: Institute for Fiscal Studies).

Draper, D.A.G., 1994, "Savings, Pension Rights, and Taxation," *De Economist,* Vol. 142 (No. 2), pp. 171–92.

Duggan, James E., Robert Gillingham, and John S. Greenlees, 1993, "The Returns Paid to Early Social Security Cohorts," Research Paper No. 9302 (Washington: United States Treasury Department).

Feldstein, Martin, 1974, "Social Security, Induced Retirement, and Aggregate Capital Accumulation," *Journal of Political Economy,* Vol. 82 (September), pp. 905–26.

———, 1977, "Social Security and Private Savings: International Evidence in an Extended Life-Cycle Model," in *The Economics of Public Services,* ed. by M. Feldstein and R. Inman (New York: Macmillan).

_____, 1982, "Social Security and Private Saving: Reply," *Journal of Political Economy,* Vol. 90 (June), pp. 630–42.

_____, 1994, *Fiscal Policies, Capital Formation, and Capitalism,* NBER Working Paper 4885 (Cambridge, Massachusetts: National Bureau of Economic Research).

_____, 1995, *Social Security and Saving: New Time Series Evidence,* NBER Working Paper 5054 (Cambridge, Massachusetts: National Bureau of Economic Research).

Gale, William G., 1995, "The Effects of Pensions on Wealth: A Reevaluation of Theory and Evidence" (unpublished; Washington: Brookings Institution).

Gillion, Colin, and Alejandro Bonilla, 1992, "Analysis of a National Private Pension Scheme: The Case of Chile," *International Labour Review,* Vol. 131 (No. 2), pp. 171–95.

Holzmann, Robert, 1995, *Pension Reform and Fiscal Stance: Financing the Transition,* FAD Seminar Series (unpublished; Washington: International Monetary Fund).

_____, 1996, "Pension Reform, Financial Market Development, and Economic Growth: Preliminary Evidence from Chile," IMF Working Paper 96/94 (Washington: International Monetary Fund).

Hsin, Ping-lung, and Olivia S. Mitchell, 1994, "The Political Economy of Public Pensions: Pension Funding, Governance, and Fiscal Stress," *Revista de Análisis Económico,* Vol. 9 (June), pp. 1511–68.

Hubbard, R. Glenn, 1986, "Pension Wealth and Individual Saving," *Journal of Money, Credit and Banking,* Vol. 18 (May), pp. 167–78.

Husain, Aasim M., 1995, "Determinants of Private Saving in Singapore," in *Singapore: A Case Study in Rapid Development,* ed. by Kenneth Bercuson, IMF Occasional Paper 119 (Washington: International Monetary Fund).

Jappelli, Tulio, 1995, "Does Social Security Reduce the Accumulation of Private Wealth? Evidence from Italian Survey Data," *Ricerche Economiche,* Vol. 49 (March), pp. 1–31.

Kopits, G., and P. Gotur, 1980, "The Influence of Social Security on Household Savings: A Cross-Country Investigation," *Staff Papers,* International Monetary Fund, Vol. 27 (March), pp. 161–90.

Koskela, E., and M. Viren, 1983, "Social Security and Household Saving in an International Cross Section," *American Economic Review,* Vol. 73 (March), pp. 212–17.

_____, 1986, "Social Security and Household Saving in an International Cross-Section: Some Further Evidence," Bank of Finland Working Paper TU 2/86 (Helsinki).

Kotlikoff, Laurence J., 1979, "Testing the Theory of Social Security and Life Cycle Accumulation," *American Economic Review,* Vol. 69 (June), pp. 396–410.

_____, and Lawrence H. Summers, 1981, "The Role of Intergenerational Transfers in Aggregate Capital Accumulation," *Journal of Political Economy,* Vol. 89 (August), pp. 706–32.

Leimer, D.R., and S. Lesnoy, 1982, "Social Security and Private Saving: New Time-Series Evidence," *Journal of Political Economy,* Vol. 90 (June), pp. 606–29.

Leimer, D.R., and David H. Richardson, 1992, "Social Security, Uncertainty Adjustments and the Consumption Decision," *Economica,* Vol. 59 (August), pp. 311–35.

Modigliani, F., and A. Sterling, 1983, "The Determinants of Private Saving with Special Reference to the Role of Social Security—Cross-Country Tests," in *The Determinants of National Savings and Wealth,* ed. by F. Modigliani and R. Hemming (New York: St. Martin's Press).

Munnell, Alicia H., 1974, *The Effect of Social Security on Personal Saving* (Cambridge, Massachusetts: Ballinger).

_____, 1976, "Private Pensions and Saving: New Evidence," *Journal of Political Economy,* Vol. 84 (October), pp. 1013–32.

_____, 1985, "Social Security, Private Pensions and Saving," in *Public Finance and Social Policy,* ed. by G. Terny and A.J. Culyer (Detroit: Wayne State University Press).

_____, 1992, "Current Taxation of Qualified Pension Plans: Has the Time Come?" *New England Economic Review,* Federal Reserve Bank of Boston (March–April), pp. 12–25.

Oudet, Bruno, 1979, "Data and Studies on Saving in France: A Survey," in *Social Security Versus Private Saving,* ed. by G. von Furstenberg, (Cambridge, Massachusetts: Ballinger).

Palmer, Edward, 1988, "Economic and Social Aspects of the Financing of Retirement Pensions in Sweden," in *Economic and Social Aspects of Social Security* (Geneva, Switzerland: International Social Security Association).

Perelman, S., and P. Pestieau, 1984, "The Effect of Social Security on Saving: The Case of Belgium with a Particular Emphasis on the Behavior of the Aged," *Empirical Economics,* Vol. 9 (No. 1), pp. 15–26.

Pitelis, Christos N., 1985, "Effects of Life Assurance and Pension Funds on Other Savings: The Postwar U.K. Experience," *Bulletin of Economic Research,* Vol. 37 (September), pp. 213–29.

Poterba, James M., Steven F. Venti, and David A. Wise, 1993, *Do 401(k) Contributions Crowd Out Other Personal Saving?* NBER Working Paper 4391 (Cambridge, Massachusetts: National Bureau of Economic Research).

Rossi, Nicola, and Ignazio Visco, 1992, "Private Saving and the Government Deficit in Italy: 1951–1990," Temi di Discussione No. 178 (Rome: Banca d'Italia).

Savastano, Miguel A., 1995, "Private Saving in IMF Arrangements," in *IMF Conditionality: Experience Under Stand-By and Extended Arrangements, Part II: Background Papers,* ed. by Susan Schadler, IMF Occasional Paper 129 (Washington: International Monetary Fund).

Schmidt-Hebbel, Klaus, 1995, "Colombia's Pension Reform: Fiscal and Macroeconomic Effects," World Bank Discussion Papers, No. 314 (Washington: World Bank).

Seldon, Arthur, 1994, "Saving for Life-Time Risks," *Economic Affairs,* Vol. 14 (October), pp. 24–26.

Shome, Parthasarathi, and Katrine Saito, 1980, "Creating Capital Through Social Security Institutions: The Asian Experience," Domestic Finance Studies, No. 61 (Washington: World Bank).

Smith, Roger S., 1990, "Factors Affecting Saving, Policy Tools, and Tax Reform: A Review," *Staff Papers,* International Monetary Fund, Vol. 37 (March), pp. 1–70.

Venti, Steven F., and David A. Wise, 1986, *IRAs and Savings,* NBER Working Paper 1879 (Cambridge, Massachusetts: National Bureau of Economic Research).

_____, 1996, "The Wealth of Cohorts: Retirement Saving and the Changing Assets of Older Americans," NBER Working Paper 5609 (Cambridge, Massachusetts: National Bureau of Economic Research).

Wallich, Christine, 1981, *Social Security and Savings Mobilization: A Case Study of Chile,* Domestic Finance Studies, No. 67 (Washington: World Bank).

Warshawsky, Mark, 1987, "Private Annuity Markets in the United States, 1919–1984," Research Papers in Banking and Financial Economics (Washington: Financial Studies Section, Division of Research and Statistics, Board of Governors of the Federal Reserve System).

Waters, William R., 1981, *Employer Pension Plan Membership and Household Wealth* (Philadelphia: University of Pennsylvania).

World Bank, 1993, "Social Security Administration Cost Study" (unpublished; Washington: Latin America and the Caribbean Regional Office, Technical Department, Public Sector Management Division).

_____, 1994, "Averting the Old Age Crisis: Policies to Protect the Old and Promote Growth," World Bank Policy Research Report (New York: Oxford University Press).

Yamada, Tetsuji, and Tadashi Yamada, 1988, *The Effects of Japanese Social Security Retirement Benefits on Personal Savings and Elderly Labor Force Behavior,* NBER Working Paper 2661 (Cambridge, Massachusetts: National Bureau of Economic Research).

_____, and Guoen Liu, 1990, *Determinants of Saving and Labor Force Participation of the Elderly in Japan,* NBER Working Paper 3292 (Cambridge, Massachusetts: National Bureau of Economic Research).

_____, 1992, "Interdependency of Personal Savings and Labour Force Participation of the Elderly, and Social Security Wealth: A Time Series Analysis," *Applied Economics,* Vol. 24 (April), pp. 379–88.

Recent Occasional Papers of the International Monetary Fund

153. Pension Regimes and Saving, by G.A. Mackenzie, Philip Gerson, and Alfredo Cuevas. 1997.

152. Hong Kong, China: Growth, Structural Change, and Economic Stability During the Transition, by John Dodsworth and Dubravko Mihaljek. 1997.

151. Currency Board Arrangements: Issues and Experiences, by a staff team led by Tomás J.T. Baliño and Charles Enoch. 1997.

150. Kuwait: From Reconstruction to Accumulation for Future Generations, by Nigel Andrew Chalk, Mohamed A. El-Erian, Susan J. Fennell, Alexei P. Kireyev, and John F. Wison. 1997.

149. The Composition of Fiscal Adjustment and Growth: Lessons from Fiscal Reforms in Eight Economies, by G.A. Mackenzie, David W.H. Orsmond, and Philip R. Gerson. 1997.

148. Nigeria: Experience with Structural Adjustment, by Gary Moser, Scott Rogers, and Reinold van Til, with Robin Kibuka and Inutu Lukonga. 1997.

147. Aging Populations and Public Pension Schemes, by Sheetal K. Chand and Albert Jaeger. 1996.

146. Thailand: The Road to Sustained Growth, by Kalpana Kochhar, Louis Dicks-Mireaux, Balazs Horvath, Mauro Mecagni, Erik Offerdal, and Jianping Zhou. 1996.

145. Exchange Rate Movements and Their Impact on Trade and Investment in the APEC Region, by Takatoshi Ito, Peter Isard, Steven Symansky, and Tamim Bayoumi. 1996.

144. National Bank of Poland: The Road to Indirect Instruments, by Piero Ugolini. 1996.

143. Adjustment for Growth: The African Experience, by Michael T. Hadjimichael, Michael Nowak, Robert Sharer, and Amor Tahari. 1996.

142. Quasi-Fiscal Operations of Public Financial Institutions, by G.A. Mackenzie and Peter Stella. 1996.

141. Monetary and Exchange System Reforms in China: An Experiment in Gradualism, by Hassanali Mehran, Marc Quintyn, Tom Nordman, and Bernard Laurens. 1996.

140. Government Reform in New Zealand, by Graham C. Scott. 1996.

139. Reinvigorating Growth in Developing Countries: Lessons from Adjustment Policies in Eight Economies, by David Goldsbrough, Sharmini Coorey, Louis Dicks-Mireaux, Balazs Horvath, Kalpana Kochhar, Mauro Mecagni, Erik Offerdal, and Jianping Zhou. 1996.

138. Aftermath of the CFA Franc Devaluation, by Jean A.P. Clément, with Johannes Mueller, Stéphane Cossé, and Jean Le Dem. 1996.

137. The Lao People's Democratic Republic: Systemic Transformation and Adjustment, edited by Ichiro Otani and Chi Do Pham. 1996.

136. Jordan: Strategy for Adjustment and Growth, edited by Edouard Maciejewski and Ahsan Mansur. 1996.

135. Vietnam: Transition to a Market Economy, by John R. Dodsworth, Erich Spitäller, Michael Braulke, Keon Hyok Lee, Kenneth Miranda, Christian Mulder, Hisanobu Shishido, and Krishna Srinivasan. 1996.

134. India: Economic Reform and Growth, by Ajai Chopra, Charles Collyns, Richard Hemming, and Karen Parker with Woosik Chu and Oliver Fratzscher. 1995.

133. Policy Experiences and Issues in the Baltics, Russia, and Other Countries of the Former Soviet Union, edited by Daniel A. Citrin and Ashok K. Lahiri. 1995.

132. Financial Fragilities in Latin America: The 1980s and 1990s, by Liliana Rojas-Suárez and Steven R. Weisbrod. 1995.

131. Capital Account Convertibility: Review of Experience and Implications for IMF Policies, by staff teams headed by Peter J. Quirk and Owen Evans. 1995.

130. Challenges to the Swedish Welfare State, by Desmond Lachman, Adam Bennett, John H. Green, Robert Hagemann, and Ramana Ramaswamy. 1995.

129. IMF Conditionality: Experience Under Stand-By and Extended Arrangements. Part II: Background Papers. Susan Schadler, Editor, with Adam Bennett, Maria Carkovic, Louis Dicks-Mireaux, Mauro Mecagni, James H.J. Morsink, and Miguel A. Savastano. 1995.

128. IMF Conditionality: Experience Under Stand-By and Extended Arrangements. Part I: Key Issues and Findings, by Susan Schadler, Adam Bennett, Maria Carkovic, Louis Dicks-Mireaux, Mauro Mecagni, James H.J. Morsink, and Miguel A. Savastano. 1995.

127. Road Maps of the Transition: The Baltics, the Czech Republic, Hungary, and Russia, by Biswajit Banerjee, Vincent Koen, Thomas Krueger, Mark S. Lutz, Michael Marrese, and Tapio O. Saavalainen. 1995.

126. The Adoption of Indirect Instruments of Monetary Policy, by a staff team headed by William E. Alexander, Tomás J.T. Baliño, and Charles Enoch. 1995.

125. United Germany: The First Five Years—Performance and Policy Issues, by Robert Corker, Robert A. Feldman, Karl Habermeier, Hari Vittas, and Tessa van der Willigen. 1995.

124. Saving Behavior and the Asset Price "Bubble" in Japan: Analytical Studies, edited by Ulrich Baumgartner and Guy Meredith. 1995.

123. Comprehensive Tax Reform: The Colombian Experience, edited by Parthasarathi Shome. 1995.

122. Capital Flows in the APEC Region, edited by Mohsin S. Khan and Carmen M. Reinhart. 1995.

121. Uganda: Adjustment with Growth, 1987–94, by Robert L. Sharer, Hema R. De Zoysa, and Calvin A. McDonald. 1995.

120. Economic Dislocation and Recovery in Lebanon, by Sena Eken, Paul Cashin, S. Nuri Erbas, Jose Martelino, and Adnan Mazarei. 1995.

119. Singapore: A Case Study in Rapid Development, edited by Kenneth Bercuson with a staff team comprising Robert G. Carling, Aasim M. Husain, Thomas Rumbaugh, and Rachel van Elkan. 1995.

118. Sub-Saharan Africa: Growth, Savings, and Investment, by Michael T. Hadjimichael, Dhaneshwar Ghura, Martin Mühleisen, Roger Nord, and E. Murat Uçer. 1995.

117. Resilience and Growth Through Sustained Adjustment: The Moroccan Experience, by Saleh M. Nsouli, Sena Eken, Klaus Enders, Van-Can Thai, Jörg Decressin, and Filippo Cartiglia, with Janet Bungay. 1995.

116. Improving the International Monetary System: Constraints and Possibilities, by Michael Mussa, Morris Goldstein, Peter B. Clark, Donald J. Mathieson, and Tamim Bayoumi. 1994.

115. Exchange Rates and Economic Fundamentals: A Framework for Analysis, by Peter B. Clark, Leonardo Bartolini, Tamim Bayoumi, and Steven Symansky. 1994.

114. Economic Reform in China: A New Phase, by Wanda Tseng, Hoe Ee Khor, Kalpana Kochhar, Dubravko Mihaljek, and David Burton. 1994.

113. Poland: The Path to a Market Economy, by Liam P. Ebrill, Ajai Chopra, Charalambos Christofides, Paul Mylonas, Inci Otker, and Gerd Schwartz. 1994.

112. The Behavior of Non-Oil Commodity Prices, by Eduardo Borensztein, Mohsin S. Khan, Carmen M. Reinhart, and Peter Wickham. 1994.

111. The Russian Federation in Transition: External Developments, by Benedicte Vibe Christensen. 1994.

110. Limiting Central Bank Credit to the Government: Theory and Practice, by Carlo Cottarelli. 1993.

109. The Path to Convertibility and Growth: The Tunisian Experience, by Saleh M. Nsouli, Sena Eken, Paul Duran, Gerwin Bell, and Zühtü Yücelik. 1993.

108. Recent Experiences with Surges in Capital Inflows, by Susan Schadler, Maria Carkovic, Adam Bennett, and Robert Kahn. 1993.

107. China at the Threshold of a Market Economy, by Michael W. Bell, Hoe Ee Khor, and Kalpana Kochhar with Jun Ma, Simon N'guiamba, and Rajiv Lall. 1993.

Note: For information on the title and availability of Occasional Papers not listed, please consult the IMF Publications Catalog or contact IMF Publication Services.